The Godward Gaze

Steve McVey

HARVEST HOUSE™PUBLISHERS

EUGENE, OREGON

Cover by Left Coast Design, Portland, Oregon

Cover photo by David Samuel Robbins/CORBIS

THE GODWARD GAZE
Copyright © 2003 by Steve McVey
Published by Harvest House Publishers
Eugene, Oregon 97402
www.harvesthousepublishers.com

Library of Congress Cataloging-in-Publication Data
McVey, Steve, 1954-
   The Godward gaze / Steve McVey.
      p. cm.
Includes bibliographical references.
   ISBN 0-7369-1151-0 (pbk.)
   1. Spiritual life—Christianity.   I. Title.
   BV4501.3.M393 2003
   231' .6—dc21   2003002447

Printed in the United States of America

03 04 05 06 07 08 09 / BP-MS / 10 9 8 7 6 5 4 3 2 1

To my sister, Jan,

who continuously brightens my life
with her sense of humor
and whose love and affirmation
have been lifelong gifts to me.

Acknowledgments

This book is part of a process that the Divine Lover has been working in my life over the past few years. I think of its contents as applied grace—the practical ways that I am learning to see the loving face of my heavenly Father more clearly.

God has placed people in my path who have greatly enriched my own journey of grace and have helped point the way. We could not have published *The Godward Gaze* without the encouraging influence of these friends. I owe a debt of gratitude to each of them.

My thanks to my friends at Harvest House Publishers. The partnership I have shared with them over the years has been one of grace personified. Besides being the consummate professionals, they are just a great group of people. Thank you, guys!

An author is blessed when friends provide a private place to get away and write. Several generous people shared such a gift as I wrote this book. Tom and Jane Knuth were godsends—they allowed me to stay in their condo at Crystal River, Florida, to write for several weeks. So were Mick and Inga Callahan, who allowed me to spend two weeks writing at their vacation home at Cedar Key, Florida. Thanks so much for your generosity. While in your homes, I was able to accomplish much as the book's deadline approached. Special appreciation also to Patrick Callahan, who made arrangements for me.

My appreciation goes to Barry Grecu, who alerted me to some key resources for growing in my own understanding of the spiritual disciplines. His encouragement and help was timely and important to me.

Special thanks to my assistant, Cheryl Buchanan, who continuously handles a myriad of details so that I can be free to focus on the things I'm called to do. I'd be a mess without her organizational skills and efficiency.

My deep love and appreciation go to my wife, Melanie. Her love, encouragement, and affirmation make me a better man in every way. The Bible asks, "An excellent wife, who can find?" I can answer that question.

Finally, my greatest gratitude goes to Jesus Christ. To acknowledge Him within a list of others risks the appearance of trivializing His place. He doesn't belong on a list. He hasn't just been a help. He is my very Life. May you, Lord Jesus, receive all glory for any good that may come from this book. Apart from You, nothing has meaning. Thank You.

Contents

A Mistaken Identity

THE POPULAR 70S TELEVISION SERIES *All in the Family* featured an episode in which Archie Bunker discovered he had accidentally locked himself in his basement on a cold winter morning. His family members were all gone for the day, and the only thing Archie could find to warm himself with was an old bottle of vodka. As the day progressed and the contents of the bottle diminished, an inebriated Archie found himself praying, asking God to help him get out of the basement before he froze to death.

Finally, late in the day, he heard a sound upstairs.

"Is that You, Lord?" he asked, now in a drunken stupor.

"Mr. Bunker? Where are you?" the voiced answered.

"I'm down here in the basement, Lord," Archie replied.

What Archie didn't know was that the voice was that of his African-American neighbor, who from outside the house had heard Archie calling for help. He had come into the house in response to his cry.

Anybody who is familiar with Archie Bunker would probably describe him as racist. On this particular occasion, the last thing Archie expected to see was an African-American coming to his rescue. In his drunken frame of mind, he was looking for God.

"I'm coming to get you, Mr. Bunker," the benevolent visitor assured him.

"Thank you, Lord," Archie answered. "I'm ready for you to take me now, Lord."

The neighbor opened the door to the basement and began to walk downstairs, where Archie was slumped over, face down. As the man reached the bottom of the stairs, Archie pushed himself up to take the hand of God and be carried away. Looking into the man's face with an expression of shock and horror, the drunken racist cried out, "Forgive me, Lord! I didn't know!"

This episode from a television sitcom, although a comedy, raises a serious question. When you see God face-to-face, will you be shocked by what you see? Each of us has formed his or her own concept of who God is based on the input we have received. The accuracy of our concept of God depends largely on whether that input was reliable and how properly we interpreted it. And make no mistake about it—*our concept of God will largely determine the way we relate to Him.*

God—the Divine Lover

What adjectives would you use to describe God? If you were to write an essay describing His character and personality, what would you write? Would your finished paper describe God in a way that would entice your reader to earnestly seek Him? Or would it make Him look more like pagan deities who must be constantly appeased? Is your God someone you must constantly pursue—and try to please—or do you see Him as One who is fully satisfied with you and constantly pursuing your company?

Many struggle to believe that God craves intimacy with them because their concept of Him has been influenced by the legalism so common in our present culture. Such a God is impossible to please—not at all like the God who sent His Son to fully satisfy all the demands of righteousness on our behalf. Still other believers are more comfortable with a safe, distant God who stays in heaven, watching over His creatures but not interacting with them in divine love.

And yet the God revealed in the Bible is always for us, always pursuing us, seeking to be our Divine Lover. Other concepts of God ultimately cause us to look away from Him. We won't *want* to look directly into His face. Instead, we will shy away from intimacy with Him because we feel afraid, ashamed, and unworthy.

The fact that you're reading a book about gazing into the face of God is evidence that you hunger to know this Divine Lover. Intimacy with Him is your passion. And this fierce desire to know Him fully—to gaze into His face—is the result of His work in your life. Not everybody has the desire you have, but your hunger for Him is undeniable.

That hunger didn't just happen. The Holy Spirit *put it there* to draw you toward God. Your heavenly Father has set His heart on you and wants to take you to a deeper level of intimacy with Him in which you gaze more fully into His face, regardless of your daily circumstances.

The Rhythms of Grace

How can we see the face of God in our daily lives? By looking toward Him in faith. The ongoing relationship between a Christian and our heavenly Father isn't based on works, but it isn't a passive lifestyle either. As we walk with Him, the Holy Spirit develops within us what Eugene Peterson calls in *The Message* "the rhythms of grace." Other writers have used the term *spiritual disciplines*. But whether we call them rhythms of grace or spiritual disciplines or some other name, these biblical practices, when motivated by love and faith, help us experience a deeper sense of intimacy with God than we could otherwise know.

Some people who appreciate God's grace may recoil from the term *spiritual discipline*. It carries a negative connotation in their minds. *Discipline* is what one does to a misbehaving child. *Discipline* may conjure up images of gritting your teeth and resolving to do something you know needs to be done, but don't want to do. One may discipline himself to say no to cheesecake and yes to exercise. When you hear the word *discipline*, you may associate it with something you *ought* to do as opposed to something you *want* to do.

However, when we understand discipline within the context of grace, we realize that speaking of the disciplines of the Christian life is like talking about the disciplines of marriage. The disciplines of marriage? Let's see…kissing, talking, dreaming together, rearing children together… these may not happen without effort, but they wouldn't be considered *discipline* in any negative sense of the word. They are all part of the rhythms of marriage. So too, when a believer walks in grace, he *wants* to do anything that might help facilitate spiritual growth or a deeper sense of intimacy with Christ.

As you read *The Godward Gaze*, don't think of the spiritual disciplines discussed here as things you *ought* to do, duties which must be fulfilled by sheer self-discipline. Instead, consider them as gifts from God—rhythms of grace that can draw you into a greater awareness of His love for you. To understand this concept, be sure to read the following chapters through lenses of grace, not of legalism.

In his now classic book *Celebration of Discipline*, Richard Foster wisely notes:

The Spiritual Disciplines are intended for our good. They are meant to bring the abundance of God into our lives. It is possible, however, to turn them into another set of soul-killing laws. Law-bound Disciplines breathe death.

As we enter the inner world of the Spiritual Disciplines, there will always be the danger of turning them into laws. But we are not left to our own human devices. Jesus Christ has promised to be our ever-present Teacher and Guide. His voice is not hard to hear. His direction is not hard to understand. If we are beginning to calcify what should always remain alive and growing, he will tell us. We can trust his teaching. If we are wandering off toward some wrong idea or unprofitable practice, he will guide us back. If we are willing to listen to the Heavenly Monitor, we will receive the instruction we need.[1]

We have not only the presence of Christ to teach us how to apply the disciplines, but also the encouragement of the apostle Paul, who advised Timothy to "discipline yourself for the purpose of godliness" (1 Timothy 4:7). Why would we do less?

The Upward Look, the Inward Look, the Outward Look

The Godward Gaze is divided into three parts. Each section focuses on a different spiritual discipline or lens through which we may gaze into the face of God. Part 1 will direct us toward "The Upward Look." These chapters will help you to grow in the ability to see His face through the lenses of awareness, quietness, and contentment.

Part 2 will point toward "The Inward Look." In this section, we will examine practical ways we can allow His love to captivate us as it moves from our head to our heart through contemplation, meditation, and identification with Him in His death and resurrection. These three disciplines will help us see the beauty of the Divine Lover.

The final part of the book will guide us toward "The Outward Look." You may be both amazed and thrilled as you learn how to hear God speak to you through the creativity found in this world, through the practice of celebration, and through your service. You will probably discover that God has been talking to you every day in a multitude of ways. Now you can learn how to better recognize His voice and understand what He is saying.

At the close of each chapter you will find practical suggestions for applying the teaching contained in that chapter. Don't just read *The Godward Gaze*. Respond to what you hear the Holy Spirit saying by acting on these suggestions at the end of each chapter. Interact with your heavenly Father and believe in faith that the Holy Spirit will minister to you at the very moment that you are responding to what you have read. Keep a notebook with this book so that you can keep your notes together as you respond to the guidelines at the end of each chapter.

LOOKING UPWARD

1. Write a one-paragraph description of God. Think about God's personality. Don't just repeat biblical words to describe Him. In other words, don't simply parrot what you've read or been told. Instead, describe your understanding of God, your relationship with Him, and His actions in your life.

2. What are the primary messages that have shaped your concept of God? For instance, what message did you receive about God from

- your family

- your church

- your culture

- the circumstances of your life

3. How have these messages helped or hurt your relationship with God? Ask your heavenly Father to
   deeply ingrain into you the truth about His personality and character and to free you from any negative effects of the lies that you may have believed
   about Him. If you can identify any lies, write them
   in your notebook. Then strike through each one and
   write the corresponding truth about God underneath
   it.

4. Envision what you would look like if the Lord turned
   you into the person you want to be.

   - What would your relationship with Him be like?

   - In what ways would you see yourself differently?

   - What Bible character would you want your life
     to most closely resemble (other than Jesus)?

   - What are the characteristics of that person's life
     that you find attractive?

   - In what ways are you least like that person right
     now?

Do you really want to change? The key to becoming all you're capable of being is to gaze into the
face of God. That's the only thing the Bible ever
plainly says will change us into the image of the Lord
Himself. The Scripture says, "But we all, with open

face as beholding in a glass the glory of the Lord, are changed into the same image from glory to glory, even as by the Spirit of the Lord" (2 Corinthians 3:18 KJV).

We received the nature of Jesus Christ within us at the moment we trusted Him. However, the work of the Holy Spirit is to cause us to mature in grace until our attitudes and actions conform with the righteousness of Christ, which already fills our spirits. That change occurs through the ongoing work of sanctification He does within us.

Self-effort will not change our lives. If that worked, most of us would already have reached perfection because we have certainly tried—and failed. What *does* change a person is a consistent Godward gaze into the beautiful face of our Divine Lover, who is more committed to us than we can imagine. Determine now to give up on self-effort and simply look to Him.

Does the following prayer express your heart's desire? If so, let it be your own.

Dear Father,

I want to know You as You really are. Cause me to see the ways that I have misunderstood You. You have promised that when we know the truth, it will set us free. I want to be free to enjoy intimacy with You to the fullest extent possible. I sincerely want to gaze into Your lovely face every day of my life. Amen.

Part One
The Upward Look

1
Awareness:
Seeing His Lovely Face

LAST WEEK WAS A MILEPOST IN MY LIFE. I finally had to give in and get contact lenses. I've known for some time now that this was coming. I started holding books farther and farther from my face as I read. I couldn't grow longer arms, and I didn't want to stop reading, so I broke down and bought reading glasses at the dollar store. I wouldn't use them in public when I spoke. I'd just lay my study notes and Bible on the pulpit and back up until I was far enough away to read them. When I found myself practically standing with the choir, I knew I had to do something.

So I did what nearly all men in their forties end up doing—I went to the optometrist. There I learned that my vision was not only unclear up close but also not so good at a distance either. I thought of all the times my wife, Melanie, had preached to me that we both would have been killed in an auto accident if she hadn't urged me to stop before I ran into the car in front of me. I had always thought she just found some sort of fleshly pride in thinking she was my guardian angel. Now I knew she had been right all along.

The optometrist experimented with different prescription strengths until she found the one that fit me. In the week that I've been wearing contacts, I've begun noticing individual leaves on trees again. I've reduced the viewing size on my computer screen from 125 percent back to 100 percent. I'm even training myself not to hold the things I read as far from my head as possible. Too bad I allowed my pride to keep me from getting the correct lenses as soon as I needed them.

With 20/20 vision I'm seeing life more clearly and enjoying it more fully. Our spiritual lives work the same way. We tend to be shortsighted. We focus on the things right in our face and often have trouble gaining a clear perspective on things eternal. We're caught up in our careers, church activities, family responsibilities, and countless other things that capture our constant attention. Gradually, our uncorrected myopia may cause us to lose sight of the most important element of life—our relationship with God through Christ.

We don't forget God, but our vision of Him in our daily lives becomes blurry. We sometimes become so focused on those things which demand our time and energy that we neglect the One who, although never demanding, loves us more than anybody else ever will or ever could. As time passes, we may lose sight of the face of God.

The Lens of Awareness

I liken the first spiritual discipline to a corrective lens through which we may more fully gaze into the loving face of God. That lens, that discipline, is *awareness*. It is a heightened recognition of our Divine Lover in our everyday lives. A certainty that God is with us in every step we take and every breath we breathe. Even now, as you read, are you vividly aware of God's presence?

We often stand in the very presence of God and fail to recognize Him. Even biblical characters were sometimes blind to His presence among them.

On the road to Emmaus the disciples walked beside Jesus, totally oblivious to the fact that the One whose death they mourned was speaking to them as they walked along (Luke 24:13-35).

At the trial of Jesus, Pilate asked, "What is truth?" And yet he was speaking to eternal truth incarnate standing 18 inches from his nose (John 18:38).

On resurrection day, Mary didn't recognize Jesus as she cried out to Him outside the empty tomb, "Sir, they have stolen His body! Please, if you know where they have taken it, tell me!" (see John 20:15).

During a violent storm, as the disciples toiled in windy weather at sea aboard a fishing boat, Jesus came walking toward them on the water. Most cried out when they saw Him, "It is a ghost!" Only one man in that boat recognized Him (Matthew 14:25-29).

These biblical characters were no different from many today who wish they could see Jesus but don't perceive His presence among them. Jesus is always here where we are. He never leaves. Our Lord is not a theological proposition—He's a Person with thoughts and feelings and desires just like ours. His greatest desire is for us to understand how much He loves us and to love Him in return. He doesn't just want us to believe He is with us. He wants us to *recognize* Him with us.

Several years ago national news broadcasts reported accounts of appearances of the Virgin Mary in a farm field in a suburb near our church. For months, people came to the field to await her appearance. From around the world they came, hoping to be there when Mary showed up to give her monthly message through a self-appointed spokesperson. Our church decided to capitalize on the situation by changing the lettering on the sign in front of our building to read, "Why drive there to see Mary? Stop here and see Jesus!"

We weren't trying to be irreverent but simply using a little humor to make the point that Jesus Christ is present with us each time we meet together. Jesus said that when two or more gather together in His name, He is there in the midst of them (Matthew 18:20). But do we really believe that? Are we *aware* of His presence—either when two or more are gathered or when we're going about our daily business?

Deterrents to Spiritual Awareness

If we're honest, we'll admit that far too often we breeze through our day merely entertaining a few passing thoughts of the Lord rather than enjoying an acute awareness of His presence. What keeps us from identifying Him in everyday matters? Several deterrents hinder our awareness of the Lord's nearness.

The Way Jesus Relates to Us

Many Christians don't recognize the Lord's continuous presence with them because He often chooses to relate to those He loves in a subtle way. Jesus is the kind of Lover that doesn't approach us in a brash and intrusive manner. He's not pushy. On rare occasions, He may suddenly overtake and ravish a person with His love as He did with the apostle Paul on the Damascus Road (Acts 9). However, His normal practice is to gently whisper to us in a still, small voice, drawing our attention and devotion toward Himself until we become so totally consumed with Him that, by comparison, everything else becomes unimportant.

For instance, as He walked with the disciples on the road from Jerusalem to Emmaus, "their eyes were prevented from recognizing Him" (Luke 24:16). When they reached the end of their seven-mile walk, Jesus "acted as though He were going farther" (24:28). Why did He do that? Like you, Jesus wants to be wanted by those He loves. Intimacy with Him is the result of an invitation, not an intrusion.

The disciples urged Him—"Stay with us," they insisted (Luke 23:29). So He did. This is typical of Jesus. First, He attracts us to Himself until we long to know Him more intimately, and then He reveals Himself to us more and more as we respond to the knowledge we already have of Him.

Our Personal Circumstances

We can easily become so preoccupied with our own circumstances that Jesus seems to get lost in the shuffle. The disciples walking the Emmaus Road with Christ were bogged down in their despair about His crucifixion. When Jesus came near them, all they could see were their seemingly adverse circumstances.

To call them shortsighted is an understatement. They could see only the superficial—the natural elements—and were blind to the supernatural. Their interpretation of life made no room for the possibility of a Divine breakthrough into their situation.

The threat to our ability to recognize Jesus is no different. Our senses are so bombarded with the details of our lives that sometimes we can barely discern Him. Have you become so caught up in the demands of daily circumstances that you've lost the consciousness of Christ? The danger is an age-old threat, known even to those who walked beside Jesus on a dusty road two millennia ago.

A Religious Lens

Surprisingly, a religious perspective can hide Jesus from us. Certainly, we can see Christ within "religious" contexts. Most believers have seen the Lord in church, Bible studies, religious books, spiritual music, and countless other religious aids. We must not devalue the ways that Christians have traditionally experienced the Lord's presence in their lives. But traditional religious means aren't the *only* ways that Christ manifests Himself to those He loves.

In Part 3 we will see that Christ will make Himself known to us in more ways than we can imagine if only we have eyes to see and ears to hear. Jesus doesn't just speak a religious language. He speaks the language of our everyday lives. Those who expect to see Him only within a religious context severely limit their ability to recognize Him. They are looking for Him through a lens with the diameter of a straw when, in reality, He is displaying a panoramic view of Himself that encompasses all of life.

My wife, Melanie, and I have enjoyed opportunities to occasionally vacation in the Caribbean. At times I have stood in scenic spots overlooking the ocean with my camera in hand. I've felt overwhelmed by the majestic beauty that surrounds me. Blue, crystal clear water stretches out to the horizon and blends into the sky. White, powdery beaches reach as far in both directions as the eye can see. Picturesque palm trees lean forward with fronds reaching out to the water as if they too desperately want to feel the lapping waves. A gentle breeze seems to promise to breathe youth into any person who will inhale its ocean fragrance. Can you picture the scene?

Now, imagine that I lift a $15 disposable camera to my face to capture the beauty. I don't want to lose this moment. I want to pull the total impact of everything I'm experiencing through that camera's lens and take it home with me on a three-by-five photograph. I want to go home, look at this picture, and feel exactly what I'm feeling as I stand on the beach at that moment.

Do you think that will happen? Of course not. A snap-shot could never do justice to the beauty. It's only a minuscule representation of what I've seen. It can only remind me of the beauty of the moment, not duplicate it. The beauty is simply bigger than any camera can capture.

That's what happens when we try to see the beauty of Jesus through a religious lens. He is the personification of God's love—a love much too big to be contained by religion. Consequently, He reveals Himself in religious *and* nonreligious ways. For instance, the Bible says that "the heavens declare the glory of God" (Psalm 19:1 KJV). Clouds aren't religious. The blue sky isn't religious. So God doesn't only communicate through church-talk, but also through cloud-talk. These are only two of His many dialects. We'll consider others in detail in chapters that follow.

Touched by a German poem written in 1050 about the love of God, Frederick Lehman wrote in my favorite hymn:

Could we with ink the oceans fill,
And were the skies of parchment made,
Were every stalk on earth a quill,
And every man a scribe by trade,
To write the love of God above,
Would drain the oceans dry,
Nor could the scroll contain the whole,
Though stretched from sky to sky.

The means by which God declares His love and presence are without limit. Many ancient saints understood themselves to be living in a "God-bathed" world. That can be immeasurably helpful for those of us who want to deeply experience intimacy with Him. Our Divine Lover reveals Himself in many ways. Jesus is whispering to you right now, every day, in a thousand ways—and many of them aren't religious. We need only to be watching and aware.

Understanding the Lord's Languages of Love

"The Lord spoke to me the other day," a friend told me recently. "And I don't make that statement very often," she continued, obviously excited that she had heard Jesus speak. This wasn't the appropriate time for me to share the truth that Jesus Christ doesn't just occasionally speak to us. He *continually* speaks to us. If Jesus loves each of us as much as the Bible says, wouldn't He want to talk to us often? Would He love us enough to die for us and give us eternal life at salvation and then say, "Okay, I'll look forward to talking to you again when you get to heaven."

Do you hear the romantic whispers of Jesus? As Christians we claim we have a relationship with Christ, and no loving relationship exists without continuous interaction. The problem isn't that He isn't speaking. The problem is that we often aren't hearing.

How then does a person become aware of the presence of Jesus Christ and hear His voice in day-to-day living? Several prerequisites are necessary for experiencing spiritual awareness.

Dissatisfied with Our Lack of Awareness

After speaking to a group about intimacy with Christ, a lady approached me and said, "I have no sense of real intimacy with Jesus Christ. What can I do?"

"Tell me more," I said.

"Well, I've been a Christian for almost 30 years," she said. "I used to be aware of the Lord's presence in my life and really enjoyed my relationship with Him. Then I began to grow cold after my children were born. I became so busy with the details of my home and work that my spiritual life slowly faded into the background. That's where I've been for several years now."

"You sound as if you've become bogged down with the demands of life," I said. "Your family and work have overshadowed your consciousness of Christ."

"That's right," she admitted.

"How do you feel about that?" I asked.

"I was okay for a while, but lately I've felt like I've missed Jesus."

"Then you're hungry to experience Him again?" I asked.

"Yes, I am," she answered. "I've been cold for a while now, but I want to enjoy my relationship with Christ the way I used to. I'm not happy these days."

As our conversation continued, I shared a truth with this woman that helped turn her discouragement into encouragement. I reminded her that, by her own description, she had been spiritually cold for quite some time and hadn't really minded or even given much thought to her condition. Now, however, she wasn't content with her spiritual dryness. What had happened to change her attitude from indifference to dissatisfaction?

It was the Holy Spirit.

If you're unhappy about where you are spiritually, you're in a good place! Dissatisfaction with the status quo is sometimes a gift from God. Becoming unhappy with where you are is often a sign that the Holy Spirit is moving you to where you want to be. Dissatisfaction can be a great catalyst for change.

Dissatisfaction motivated Israel to follow Moses out of Egypt. Dissatisfaction spurred Nehemiah to rebuild the walls around Jerusalem. Dissatisfaction caused a rebellious son to get up from a pigpen and go home to his father. It caused one man to climb a tree and find his salvation when Jesus passed by. Dissatisfaction prompted bumbling disciples to ask Jesus, "Teach us to pray." Yes, dissatisfaction is often the prelude to supernatural changes in people's lives.

Are you dissatisfied? Congratulations! God has already begun a work in you. You wouldn't even care if He wasn't active in your life. Your dissatisfaction with where you are spiritually is evidence of God working in you to heighten your continual awareness of Him. The very fact you're dissatisfied is evidence that God is being proactive in your life at this very moment!

Pause in your reading for a minute. Acknowledge to Him the truth you have just read. Thank Him for creating this dissatisfaction within you because it's the salt that stimulates thirst for God. Do you want to recognize Jesus Christ? See Him right now in the dissatisfaction of your life.

A Hunger to Experience Christ More Intimately

Continual awareness of Christ in our daily life is inseparable from a hunger to know Him. Ask Him to make Himself known to you, and He will eagerly respond. Christians often pray for the Lord to help them to love Him more, but the way we grow in our love for Him is to grow in our understanding of His love for us. "We love Him, because He first loved us" (1 John 4:19 KJV). Our love for Christ isn't something we can work up or pray down. It's simply a response to His love.

The Lay's Potato Chip company was hugely successful with their catchy slogan, "Bet you can't eat just one!" They knew that eating one of their chips would create a hunger for more. Our relationship with Jesus Christ is like that. The psalmist said, "Oh taste and see that the LORD is good!" (Psalm 34:8). Once we have encountered His love up close and personal, we become addicted for life. We just can't get enough of Him. As Jesus reveals Himself to us, we find ourselves hungering to know Him more intimately and love Him more earnestly. Speaking from his own experience, St. Augustine said, "You flashed, You shone; and You chased away my blindness. You became fragrant; and I inhaled and sighed for You. I tasted, and now hunger and thirst for You. You touched me; and I burned for Your embrace."[2]

Spiritual hunger is the result of encountering Christ in our lives. That hunger then becomes the bridge by which we gain a heightened awareness of Him with us in our circumstances. Spiritual hunger will cause us to raise our spiritual antenna, looking for signals of His presence nearby.

Ask the Lord to reach into your life like He did into Augustine's. Then patiently wait for Him to flash, to shine, and to chase away your own blindness to His presence. He will come to you and do just that.

Remember that cultivating a spiritual hunger isn't something *you* do. It's a sovereign work of God that *He* does because He wants to constantly enjoy intimate moments with you. Be careful not to turn this into a legalistic effort to try to accomplish something spiritually productive. Ministers sometimes suggest that we must do certain things in order to experience the fullness of Christ in our lives, but the Bible teaches to the contrary.

God promises in Scripture, "I will pour water on him that is thirsty" (Isaiah 44:3 KJV). We aren't the cause of any good aspect of our walk with Christ. We are simply the recipients of every good thing that He does in our lives. "Open your mouth wide and *I* will fill it" (Psalm 81:10), promises the Lord.

Are you hungry? Open your mouth—*wide.* Remember, nobody ever came to Jesus hungry and went away that way. Jesus once asked, "What man is there among you who, when his son asks for a loaf, will give him a stone? Or if he asks for a fish, he will not give him a snake, will he?" Then the Lord promised, "If you then, being evil, know how to give good gifts to your children, how much more will your Father who is in heaven give what is good to those who ask Him?" (Matthew 7:9-11). You can be sure that your search for intimacy with Christ won't be disappointed. He can't resist a person who is spiritually hungry. Are you hungry for intimacy with Him? Just ask.

The first lens, the first spiritual discipline through which we learn to gaze into the loving face of God, is awareness. How can we cooperate with the Lord as He develops this quality in our lives? The following exercises may help.

LOOKING UPWARD

1. Pray right now and ask the Lord to give you a supernatural awareness of Him in your daily life.

    The Lord opened the eyes of the disciples on the road to Emmaus so that they became aware of Him. He can do the same for you. Your heavenly Father wants you to enjoy intimacy with Him at every moment of your life. He doesn't live at your church. He lives inside you and wants the two of you to share your life together every day. Talk to Him about your desire to recognize Him in your daily life.

2. Ask the Lord to show you the things that distract you from an awareness of His presence. List them in your notebook.

    Come back to this list each time you pray as you read this book. The list may grow as you progress through the book. When you finish this book, bring the list back to the Lord and ask Him about each item you have recorded. Do you need to put the distraction out of your life? Or do you simply need to give it the appropriate place of importance in your life? Wait for your heavenly Father to show you how to deal with the items you have listed.

3. Identify the areas of dissatisfaction in your life and talk to your Father about them.

    Don't be bashful about being honest with God. He knows you better than you know yourself. You can't say anything to Him that He doesn't already know about, so be completely honest. Jesus Christ wants to be the source of life in every part of your life. Give each area of dissatisfaction to Him and ask Him to breathe His life into that part of your life. Thank Him for your dissatisfaction because it is the salt that has made you thirsty for Him. After you have prayed, wait in silence to give Him the chance to speak to you or show you something about what you asked.

Awareness is the foundation for the rhythms of grace. Every other spiritual discipline stands on the shoulders of spiritual awareness. Seeing the lovely face of our heavenly Father is wonderful, but more awaits you. He is looking deeply into your eyes at this very moment and whispering something personal to you. How can you hear what He is saying? The answer is in the next chapter.

Dear Father,

Make me aware of You in the daily details of my life. Reveal to me the things that distract me from You and tell me how to respond to what You show me. I don't want anything to block my vision of You. I want to see you, Lord. I want to know You better every day. Amen.

2

Quietness:
Hearing Our Lover's Voice

WHEN WE LOOK THROUGH THE LENS OF AWARENESS, we see a God who has given all to win us back to Himself. Our awareness of Him includes an awareness of His passion for us. And that divine passion that Jesus Christ has for each of us is so intense and immense that He can't restrain Himself from broadcasting it across the universe. If your mental image of Jesus is of a reserved, quiet-mannered, and introverted person, you had better take a closer look. Jesus is anything but emotionally closed.

During His incarnation, Jesus openly expressed Himself, revealing a full range of emotions. At times he openly cried (John 11:35). At other times He expressed anger (Mark 11:15-16). When He saw the great needs of the multitudes, He was moved with compassion (Matthew 9:36). He even used what might be understood as sarcasm when He referred to the evil King Herod as "that fox" (Luke 13:31-32). Jesus had no problem communicating whatever He was feeling at the moment. He wasn't controlled by His emotions, but neither did He squelch them.

Lovers must learn *openness,* an ability to clearly artic-
ulate and enthusiastically communicate their feelings for
each other. Solomon, the wisest man who ever lived, taught
that a husband should be *"exhilarated* always with [his
wife's] love" (Proverbs 5:19, emphasis added). Love is
meant to touch us in the deepest places. We don't live *by*
our emotions, but living *with* them is the only way to have
a fun, fulfilling relationship.

Every marriage counselor has heard complaints from
wives about their husbands' inability or unwillingness to
express love romantically. When we are loved, we need
to *feel* loved or else the relationship becomes nothing more
than an intellectual agreement. Love restricted to the intel-
lect may not be love at all.

Love simply isn't meant to be primarily an intellectual
agreement between two people. Love is inspirational, moti-
vational, and especially *transformational* because love
changes people. Healthy love is medicine to the mind and
emotions. It builds up by being patient, supportive, kind,
and affirming (1 Corinthians 13). This is especially true of
God and His love for us.

Opening Our Ears and Listening

Jesus Christ relates to His bride, the church, as the ultimate romantic. He has no intention of leaving you wondering about His love for you. In the previous chapter we
saw the importance of developing an awareness of His
presence with us in our daily routine. Awareness is an
essential lens for gazing on the loving face of God.
However, we would do well to cultivate another spiritual
discipline if we want to enjoy intimacy with Jesus Christ.
This discipline is listening to His lovely voice in *quietness.*
To know we are loved is wonderful, but it usually isn't
enough to satisfy us. We want to *hear* it. We want love
to be spoken to us.

In addition to being aware of our Lord's presence, we need to hear His voice and understand what He is communicating to us. Jesus is continuously declaring His love for each of us, but what practical good does that do if we don't hear Him? In the book of Revelation, Jesus speaks to the believers in the churches in Asia Minor. Eight times He tells them, "He who has an ear, let Him hear what the Spirit says to the churches." He extends the same loving encouragement to us today. If you have an ear to hear, you will hear His voice.

One incident that demonstrates the importance of listening to Him in quietness occurred when God the Father spoke audibly just before Jesus went to the upper room with His disciples. Jesus was foretelling His soon approaching crucifixion. John describes the scene:

> "Now My soul has become troubled; and what shall I say, 'Father, save me from this hour'? But for this purpose I came to this hour. Father, glorify Your name." Then a voice came out of heaven: "I have both glorified it, and will glorify it again." So the crowd of people who stood by and heard it were saying that it had thundered; others were saying, "An angel has spoken to Him." Jesus answered and said, "This voice has not come for My sake, but for your sakes" (John 12:27-30).

Amazingly, people can witness the same event and come away with totally different perspectives of what happened. In this instance, God spoke audibly. Everybody agreed that they heard *something*. What they couldn't agree on was what they heard. One group said it was thunder and the other said it was an angel.

Both groups were wrong. According to Jesus, God spoke for their sakes, but they missed it. Can you imagine God speaking to you and you not realizing that what you're hearing is Him? Don't be too harsh on this crowd because each of us seems to have our own problems distinguishing the voice of God from the thunder rolling around us.

Remember, God doesn't reveal Himself only in a religious context. During His three-year public ministry, Jesus communicated God's message to people using the everyday experiences and familiar objects of their lives.

Speaking to fishermen, Jesus used fishing as a metaphor to explain God's plan for their lives (Matthew 4:19). When He was with farmers, He pointed to the crop fields to show them that God's harvest was ready (John 4:35-38). He seemed to suggest that God can speak to us through everything around us. In just one chapter (Matthew 13), Jesus referred to seeds, birds, rocks, thorns, wheat, tares, leaven, the harvest, hidden treasure, fine pearls, and a fishing net to help the disciples hear God's voice. Each was an integral part of their lives and the culture in which they lived. God spoke their language.

Although He attended the temple, Jesus never told His disciples that they had to be there to hear from God. Of course, God speaks when we come together as His church. However, He isn't limited to speaking only then and there. As Jesus demonstrated, God wants to speak to us every day through the language of our daily lives and culture. Don't wait until you get to church to hear from Him. Ask Him to open your ears to hear the melody of love He continuously sings to you. The theme of the song is always the same, but He brings it to those He loves in many different tunes.

God's Favorite Song

Jesus is not only speaking to those He loves today but actually *singing* sweet love songs to us! The Bible says that "He will rejoice over you with singing" (Zephaniah 3:17 NKJV). The New American Bible says that "He will sing joyfully *because of you.*" If you desire to experience deeper intimacy with Jesus Christ, open your heart as He sings of the deep love He has for you.

The Bible says a great deal about singing, but Zephaniah 3:17 and Psalm 32:7 are places where Scripture says *God* sings. Only twice does God let us know that He sings, and He tells us that He is singing to us! If God is singing to us, He must want us to hear what He is singing.

The Bible repeatedly shows that we can hear God in the still quietness of nature. The psalmist said that "the voice of the Lord is upon the waters" (Psalm 29:3). "The Lord thundered from heaven; the voice of the Most High resounded" (Psalm 18:13 NIV). He said that the skies are telling us about the glory of God, that "day after day they continue to speak; night after night they make Him known" (Psalm 19:1-2 NLT). Isaiah said that "the mountains and the hills will break forth into shouts of joy before you, and all the trees of the field will clap their hands" (Isaiah 55:12).

We often exclaim over a beautiful natural sight and *see* God in His handiwork, but how often do we listen to *hear* God speak through nature? Alone with God in some natural setting, we can hear nature participating in an ongoing sing-along with God as He zealously declares His love for us.

I once heard a professor ask his class, "Do you *really* believe the Bible? Have you ever heard a mountain sing or a tree clap its hands?" Though his question stemmed from cynicism, it's a good one. Have *you* heard a mountain singing or a tree clapping? Nature does indeed resound with the voice of God, but we must develop the discipline of listening, of having ears to hear.

The professor's problem was that he didn't understand that God sings through mountains and trees and everything else in nature. He thought in terms of listening with one's *physical* ears, and nobody can hear Him that way. We can't hear an FM radio broadcast with an AM receiver. Just because you don't hear it doesn't mean it isn't being played! The problem is that you aren't tuned in to the right carrier.

We've all heard the perplexing question, If a tree falls in the forest and nobody is there to hear it, does it make a sound? But let's recast that question this way: If the mountains sing and the trees clap their hands to declare the presence of God and nobody listens, does that mean the mountains' melody and the trees' joyous applause cease?

No! God's voice continues through nature whether we listen or not. The difference is that when we don't have ears to hear, we lose. We miss out on a divinely appointed provision for more intimacy with Him. We miss out on hearing His love for us resounding through His creation.

Have you heard the Divine Lover sing to you in the quietness of nature? In modern society, where people often don't venture outside the concrete jungle, a faint song in the distance beckons those with ears to hear to "come away by yourselves to a secluded place and rest a while" (Mark 6:31).

That faint song is for you.

A Personal Song

The song your Divine Lover sings to you will be the one that He knows will thrill you the most, causing you to eagerly receive His love. When Jesus Christ sings a personal song to you, the experience transforms your life. Recently I experienced such a moment myself.

I had been struggling with our ministry's financial challenges. Opportunities for the ministry to expand were opening up around the world to an extent beyond anything I had imagined. But many of the opportunities were in poor countries, and the expansion would be expensive. The doors of opportunity were opening wider, but the income to the ministry wasn't increasing. I had been praying about what to do but hadn't heard anything from heaven.

When the Divine Lover's song began, I was in Mexico, where I had been speaking at a conference. Melanie and I were driving down a coastal road one evening at sunset. As we glanced across the Bay of Banderas, the sky was a brilliant canvas of deep shades of blue, red, and pink. I soon found a spot where we pulled off the side of the road, got out of our car, and stood near the edge of a precipice where the waves crashed on the rocks below us. As we stood holding hands and staring at the horizon, I began to see a pattern in the shapes and shades of the clouds and the rays of the sun that had dipped below the horizon. The scene looked like a masterful painting, stretching all the way from one end of the horizon to the other.

"Look," I said to Melanie. "It looks like a river flowing through the middle of a desert. Can you see it? There's the blue water right in the center, and the small clouds on each side look like scrub brush along the river's edge."

"Yes, I see it too," Melanie answered. "It's beautiful."

We stood there for 20 minutes, watching the clouds all around us change colors until darkness began to fall across the river and plants in our celestial desert scene.

I didn't think about what we had seen anymore until I went to sleep that night. As I slept, I dreamed that I was again standing at that place, looking at the desert scene painted in the sky by the Divine Artist. However, unlike my waking moments there, in the dream I understood a spiritual reality.

What do you see? I heard the Lord ask as I watched the sunset in my sleep.

It's a river, I answered.

Where is it? I heard the Painter ask.

In the desert, I responded.

Suddenly a memory came to mind, and my heart was filled with joy. I began to cry and awakened with tears on my cheeks. I suddenly knew the sunset had been a love song to me.

This is the introduction to the love song: In 1994, Melanie and I wrestled with the decision to leave our local church pastorate and launch out into an itinerant ministry. We were both nervous, if not outright scared. We would be leaving a church that provided a regular income for our family. We would be stepping out in faith that God would indeed provide for our needs.

I wish I could say that we made the transition with feelings of great faith, but that isn't what happened. Our children were all still at home, and I didn't want them to suffer because of my decision. We had just built a new house, and I sometimes imagined a foreclosure notice in my hand. I also didn't want my wife to suffer a financial loss caused by a decision that I was labeling *faith*.

I assessed the situation and made my decision: *This will not work. How can God be leading me to do this? I can not survive financially if I make this move.* That was my defense and my attempt to rationalize that God couldn't be directing me to make such a financially irresponsible move.

But the inner pull to make the change wouldn't go away. Finally, we decided we would each go away for a few nights, separate from each other, to pray and seek to settle once and for all whether God was indeed leading us to leave the church pastorate. Miraculously, the Lord spoke to us both from the same Bible verse. The verse ignited faith in us to believe God and consequently to make the move.

The verse says: "Remember ye not the former things, neither consider the things of old. Behold, I will do a new thing; now it shall spring forth; shall ye not know it? *I will even make a way* in the wilderness, and *rivers* in the desert" (Isaiah 43:18-19 KJV, emphasis added).

That was all we needed. The next Sunday I resigned my position. God had told us plainly that He would make a way where none existed.

Now we were in Mexico years later, and the Lord put me on the side of a cliff, overlooking a beautiful ocean and panoramic view of the brilliant sky. As I stood there, He unveiled a painting for me, stretching across the horizon as far as I could see. What was the painting? A river in the desert. My Divine Lover was singing to me, celebrating His love over me and reminding me of the promise He had made. "I will make a way in the wilderness." Once again, I *knew* what the Lord had told me years earlier. He loves me and will always make a way. Oh, how I love that song!

If you want to experience deeper intimacy with God, then you must be open to a new sense of experiencing Him. Realize that He may sing His love to you in ways that are new to you. I recognize the danger of building our lives around subjective experiences and will readily admit that theology is proven not by experience but only by God's Word. However, many, in their desire for caution, have thrown out the baby with the bathwater.

Experience isn't the basis for our beliefs, but we shouldn't be afraid to experience God in ways that touch us emotionally. Experiencing God's interaction in your life is good and right. Christianity isn't simply a course on the subject of Christ—it's a living love story. The extremes in the modern church may be in part a reaction of believers who have found little room in traditional church settings to experience the love of God in personal ways, such as the discipline of listening to God in quietness.

Christianity is not just a religion of belief and behavior. These certainly have their place, but authentic Christianity is primarily a *relationship*. No meaningful love relationship exists apart from continuous shared experiences.

God will never reveal Himself to you in a way that contradicts what the Bible teaches, but He is more than willing to sing songs of love to you in a myriad of ways that show His creativity. Do you want to hear? Don't try to tell Him *how* He must speak to you. Find a quiet place and let Him surprise you with His love.

Paradise Lost

The Bible teaches that the goal of a Christian should be to "live peaceful and *quiet* lives in all godliness and holiness" (2 Timothy 2:2 NIV, emphasis added). In fact, we're instructed to seek earnestly to lead a quiet life (1 Thessalonians 4:11). Quietness is almost obsolete in the typical lifestyle of our day, yet only by intentionally setting aside a time and quiet place to actively listen will we hear the song He sings to us.

Ancient Christians lived in a culture that was often conducive to quiet reflection. Fewer demands competed for their time and attention. Some of us can barely remember the precious commodity of "free time."

Henri Nouwen writes about our noisy world:

> It is clear that we are usually surrounded with so much inner and outer noise that it is hard to truly hear our God when God is speaking to us. We have often become deaf, unable to know when God calls us and unable to understand in which direction God calls us. Thus our lives have become absurd. In the word "absurd" we find the Latin word *surdus,* which means "deaf."[1]

If you think of life as a river and the demands upon us for our time and energy as the current of that river, you quickly realize that the current is stronger in our day than it's ever been. Many of us grew up in a home where mom was home with the children all day, dad worked eight hours and then came home, and the demands of his day were pretty much finished. And the children? Most baby boomers can remember offering up a regular complaint to their parents: "I'm bored!" To which the unwelcome response was usually, "Clean your room" or "Mow the lawn," neither one the alternative we were looking for at the moment.

That world is no more. Today's dads often long for the good old days of a 40-hour work week. Today's moms have joined the workforce in addition to maintaining their responsibilities of childcare, housework, and countless other family tasks. And the children? They can choose from multiplex theaters with 22 screens, Nintendo, DVDs, mp3 players, and computers that offer the chance to download thousands of songs, pictures, and movies.

What is the Christian to do who wants quiet intimacy with Jesus Christ? We must *choose* quietness. We must stand against the current of our culture. Jesus Himself often made that choice. One day, after a heavy teaching ministry, He sat by the sea (Matthew 13:1). When Jesus heard about the death of John the Baptist, "He withdrew from there in a boat to a secluded place by Himself" (Matthew 14:13). When He went to the Garden of Gethsemene with His disciples, Jesus knew that His crucifixion was imminent. The Bible says that He withdrew from the disciples and knelt down to pray (Luke 22:41). Numerous times the Bible records that Jesus separated Himself from others to be alone. Even Jesus seemed to find quietness in nature to be nurturing in some way.

The apostle Paul was perhaps the most powerful minister in the history of Christianity. The Bible records that He spent three years in seclusion in a desert in Arabia (Galatians 1:15-17). Why did God pull Paul away from others and keep him only to Himself? To transform him.

Henri Nouwen also wrote:

> In solitude we can listen to the voice of the One who spoke to us before we could speak a word, who healed us before we could make any gesture to help, who set us free long before we could free others, and who loved us long before we could give love to anyone. It is in

> this solitude that we discover that being is more
> important than having, and that we are worth
> more than the result of our efforts.[2]

Do you sense an inner stirring to withdraw from the busy demands of life and meet Jesus Christ in a quiet place? Your *mind* may protest because of responsibilities and schedules, but does your *heart* hear the Divine invitation? If time were no problem, would aloneness with Jesus be appealing? If so, you can be assured that you're hearing the gentle voice of your Divine Lover inviting you to come away with Him for a while. Don't allow your head to beat your heart into submission. Follow your heart, for out of it come the issues of life (Proverbs 4:23 KJV).

If He is gently speaking to you right now, don't be like those who mistook the voice of God for thunder or an angel. If you don't sense an inner desire being stirred at this point, don't worry. Future chapters will address other ways the Lord can lovingly interact with you.

But for those who hear His call to quietness, the suggestions below may help facilitate your encounter with Him. These suggestions can lead to a romantic rendezvous between you and the Divine Lover. If you sense within your heart that He is inviting you, say yes!

You won't be disappointed.

LOOKING UPWARD

1. Set aside time in your schedule for a private rendezvous with the Divine Lover.

   This step is the hardest one to take. Maybe a glance at your calendar will suggest that you are simply too busy for such a time. This could be a wake-up call for you. The Holy Spirit may be using your full calendar to sound the alarm concerning how much you are doing.

Look at the things you have scheduled for the next 90 days. Which ones are indispensable? Which ones can be moved to a later date in order to allow you to move forward at a more leisurely pace, making time for Jesus Christ? Which activities are planned that aren't really necessary?

If your first impulse tells you that you just can't change anything, then answer one final question. What would you do if a life-threatening family emergency suddenly arose? The fact is that the value we place on things is all a matter of perspective. So go ahead. Ask the Lord to give you courage to reschedule or even scratch some of the things from your calendar.

2. Pick a meeting place where you will spend time alone with Him.

Select a place away from the hustle and bustle of your daily life. Choose a spot far enough away that you won't be tempted to jump back into the stream of normal activity after you get there. Find a place where you can be totally immersed in silence and can hear none of the sounds of modern life. A state park or nearby campground is often a good place for solitude. Most people live no more than a few hours drive from such a place.

3. Begin to prepare your heart and mind for this time.

Before your retreat, ask the Holy Spirit to guide your thoughts and to begin to show you the things He wants to deal with during your holy hideaway. Keep a pad handy and write down the things He shows you before you go. This isn't an intellectual exercise in which you write down the things that *you* want to accomplish during this time. God is in charge, not you. Ask *Him* what He wants from the time. If nothing comes to mind, don't worry. Let His agenda be a surprise.

You will likely discover that the things He wants to deal with will all be *relational* issues. Don't expect Him to take you out into the woods and give you a game plan for succeeding in business or a blueprint for being a better manager of the circumstances in your life. This time will be a time when He expresses love *to* you and stirs up love *within* you. This isn't a project to accomplish but a love rendezvous where you "waste time" with Jesus Christ and then come home renewed.

4. At the appointed time, leave everything behind and go to your chosen place.

Other than necessary personal items, take only your Bible and a notepad with you. Turn off your cell phone or leave it at home if you will be tempted to use it. One purpose in going away is to withdraw from everything else so that Jesus Christ will have your full attention.

5. Acclimate to your environment.

Modern culture batters most people's senses. You may have arrived at your private retreat location physically, but your thoughts and emotions may take a little while to catch up. Find an isolated place and slowly stroll or simply sit in silence. Feel the air and allow it to be the breath of God that gently blows away your cares. Listen intently to the sounds of nature. Watch and listen. Wait in silence and become fully present to the moment. Don't try to manipulate your feelings. Let Him be in charge.

6. Listen for His loving voice.

As you decompress from the pressure of normal daily routine, you will find a growing sense of anticipation about what Jesus will say and do as you wait to hear Him in this solitary place. When you do hear Him, respond. Write in your notebook what He shows and tells you.

In chapter 4 you will find specific guidelines on how to make the mental adjustments that allow you to give your undivided attention to Him. The key element is to wait on the Lord. Believe that He is working in you, transforming you by grace into His image.

Quiet retreats alone in nature can profoundly change your life. After you have been alone with Christ in this kind of setting on a number of occasions, you'll begin to hunger for them. Actually, the indwelling Christ within you is desiring time alone with you. *His* hunger for *you* is what you're sensing.

When you do become aware of His desire to be with you, you'll find that you begin to hunger to be alone with Him too. That's the way lovers are, even when one of them is God. He uses these desires to extend an invitation to you to come away with Him to a place where you and He can sing the songs of your heart to each other.

Dear Father,

Many voices compete for my attention, but I want to hear You. Regular quietness is foreign to me, but I recognize the value of being alone with You in a quiet place. Give me the wisdom to know how to realign my priorities to allow periods of sanctified silence. Give me the courage to act on what You show me to do. I want to hear everything that You have to say to me. Speak, Lord. I am listening. Amen.

3

Contentment:
Living from a Satisfied Heart

"GOOD MORNING, GLENDA! IT'S A BEAUTIFUL DAY, isn't it?"
Thus began my conversation with a lady at church who
seemed to be in a bad mood every time I saw her. I
couldn't remember ever hearing her say a positive word
since the day I had met her. Getting an upbeat word out
of Glenda had become a sort of challenge to me. I knew
I could find some way to get her to crack a smile and say
something positive, but so far I hadn't been successful.

This time I had seen her coming, and I just knew I'd
get a positive response. After all, this really *was* a beautiful spring day! She didn't answer the first time I spoke,
so as we approached each other in the parking lot of the
church, I pressed the matter. "Isn't this weather great?" I
asked again.

In her typical sulky voice, she responded, "They said
on TV it's supposed to start raining tomorrow morning."

I give up, I said to myself. *Putting her in a good mood
would take a miracle.*

Have you noticed that some people always seem to be content with life, while others have an uncanny capacity for finding reasons to be unsettled about the world around them? The Bible teaches that contentment brings great benefit to godly people's lives (1 Timothy 6:6).

A contented heart is a heart at peace. It's the main ingredient in the lives of those who live with an underlying sense of well-being. Contentment is an inner stillness caused by knowing our lives are firmly on the course God has set for us. Contentment is the opposite of restlessness.

The discipline of contentment is indispensable as we learn to gaze into the face of our loving God. As a believer, contentment is your birthright. If you want an unobstructed view in your own Godward gaze, look through the lens of contentment to find an intimacy that restless Christians can never know.

Impediments to Contentment

We live in a discontented world, and yet the hunger for an abiding sense of satisfaction is universal. However, we cannot find contentment apart from Jesus Christ. Instead, all that we can find is an endless variety of substitutes—counterfeit sources of contentment that gratify but never satisfy.

Many Christians have fallen into this same chase for contentment. We often look to this world in our attempt to fill our hearts with peace. Have you traveled any of the following dead-end roads?

Happiness Is Not Contentment

Many people believe that if they can just have enough (possessions), do enough (pleasures) and be enough (prestige), they will be content. These three goals have become a secular trinity in our day, but they have only brought cynicism and emptiness. *LI—FR—Jo Happiness, Pursuit*
Malcolm Muggeridge comments on this in his work *Jesus Rediscovered:*   *of = Foolish*

Muggeridge

> The pursuit of happiness, included along
> with life and liberty in the American Declaration
> of Independence as an inalienable right, is with-
> out question the most fatuous that could possi-
> bly be undertaken. This lamentable phrase—the
> pursuit of happiness—is responsible for a good
> part of the ills of the modern world.[1]

Happiness can be a shallow and illusive goal for the Christian. Certainly, nothing is wrong with being happy. In fact, happiness is commended in the Bible, but it's not guaranteed as a lifelong circumstance for any believer. To the contrary, Jesus said that in the world we will have tribulation (John 16:33). Unbroken happiness is not a God-given right. The *pursuit* of happiness is a *constitutional* right, but when a person believes that being happy all the time is his God-given right, he will never know consistent contentment.

Making happiness our greatest goal in life can lead us to believe that when we are happy, we are walking in victory, but if we are unhappy, then something is wrong with our faith. This is a dangerous teaching because nobody will experience happiness in this world all the time. Even Jesus didn't.

The Bible predicted that the Messiah would be "a man of sorrows, and acquainted with grief" (Isaiah 53:3). That prophecy came true. In the Garden of Gethsemane, Scripture says about Jesus, that "being in agony, he prayed …" (Luke 22:44 NIV). He even told His disciples, "My soul is deeply grieved, to the point of death" (Matthew 26:38). If Jesus wasn't happy all the time, we shouldn't think that we will be either.

The root of the word *happiness* comes from the old English word *hap*. It is a word that points toward circumstances. Happiness comes from happenings. We would be unrealistic to think that the happenings of life will always be to our liking.

Are Christians a happy people? Sometimes—like any-body else. Are we *always* happy? Absolutely not. However, we who know Christ have something available to us the world at large cannot know. It is something that shows what a transitory and shallow feeling happiness actually is. This "something" available to us through Jesus Christ is *joy*.

Joy is the mother of the spiritual discipline of con-tentment. It's the result of realizing that fulfillment in life doesn't depend on the external circumstances around us but resides in the eternal relationship we have with Jesus Christ. Happiness is nice, but it's sporadic. Joy, however, is continuous because its source never changes (Malachi 3:6).

Some churches glamorize happiness and question a person's faith if he expresses any sorrow or unhappiness. Don't be duped into believing that happiness is the sign of faith. It isn't.

Success Does Not Bring Contentment

American culture has deified measurable success. People today are driven to have and be the biggest and best, but they are chasing illusions. Success is relative to whatever standard of comparison is being used at the time.

Even when we do have the biggest or best in compar-ison to others, an inner voice of restlessness continues to ask if we have the biggest or best *possible*. Thus the quest for Camelot continues. We soon discover it's only a story.

The futile struggle to be all and have all will blind us to the presence of Jesus Christ in our midst. Contentment is found in Him alone, not in worldly success. First John 2:16 says, "For all that is in the world, the lust of the flesh [pleasures] and the lust of the eyes [possessions] and the boastful pride of life [prestige], is not from the Father, but is from the world."

To practice the discipline of contentment, we must be set free from an all-consuming desire to continue to achieve and attain. A man still can't serve two masters (Luke 16:13). Real contentment comes with spiritual depth, not superficial breadth.

That isn't to say that breadth is irrelevant or that God doesn't take delight in blessing His children in measurable ways. But that's His business. Our focus is to be on Christ and exploring the depths of our life in Him. Recognizing Jesus with us is impossible when we are more focused on how we can get ahead than anything else.

Does this mean that we are to become reclusive? That we are to become passive, with no regard for results? Not at all. Rather, Jesus Christ is to be the standard by which everything in our lives is evaluated. Contentment comes when our relationship with Christ becomes the lens through which we understand all of life. C.S. Lewis once said, "I believe in Christianity as I believe that the sun has risen, not only because I see it, but because by it I see everything else."[2]

Contentment never comes to those who are slaves to lust for success. When John Rockefeller was asked, "How much money is enough?" his answer was, "A little more."

Contentment, right where we are, is a great blessing.

A scene from an old TV program illustrates the point well. This conversation between Jed Clampett and Cousin Pearl took place in the television program *The Beverly Hillbillies* right after Jed discovered he had struck oil on his land.

> Jed: Pearl, what d'ya think? Think I oughta move?
>
> Pearl: Jed, how can ya even ask? Look around ya. Yore eight miles from yore nearest neighbor. Yore overrun with skunks, possums, coyotes, and bobcats. You use kerosene lamps fer light and you cook on a wood stove summer and winter. Yore drinkin' homemade moonshine

and washin' with homemade lye soap. And yore
bathroom is 50 feet from the house, and you
ask, "Should I move?"

    Jed: I reckon yore right. A man'd be a dang
fool to leave all this![3]

Distractions Can Keep Us from Contentment

Another dead-end road that will never lead to contentment has to do with how we spend our time each day.
Practically everything in our culture is designed to attract
our attention. Marketing experts know that when they get
your undivided attention, they're only a short step away
from making a sale.

Attention is a prerequisite to affection, which in turn
leads to allegiance. Anything that can continually hold our
attention will ultimately win our allegiance. The hit television programs are the ones that hold the attention of
viewers week after week.

Melanie and I have never been TV addicts, but some
time ago we came across a particular program that captured
our attention. We first saw the program on a plane and
were drawn in by its humor. When we got home, we
checked our television listing to find out when the program
aired. Before long, we found ourselves planning our
personal schedules around that program. Our initial attention to the program produced an affection that gradually
evolved into allegiance. We wouldn't even answer the
phone when the program was on the air. My level of
commitment to a TV program surprised me.

Many voices in our culture compete for our allegiance.
Each one asks us to stop, take notice, and then buy in.
Occasionally we will rearrange our lives, proving our
loyalty to these enticements that seduce us to spend all
our time and energy on them. When this happens, we have
nothing left to offer Christ.

In our culture, voices without end call out to us, vying
for our loyalty. If we aren't careful, we may become so

loyal to other things that we lose sight of our true identity. Our self-perception subtly shifts. Instead of seeing ourselves foremost as Christians, we begin to see ourselves as sports fans, businessmen, soccer moms, college students, church workers, or a thousand other identities. These compete with our understanding that we are, above all, *Christians* who are to live in the constant awareness of Christ.

How do you describe yourself? Does the word *Christian* immediately come to mind? Whatever word first pops into your head can probably give you a clue to the voices that distract you from Jesus Christ. These voices aren't necessarily evil, but our *response* to the voices may be wrong. To respond to *some* of the voices that call out to us is normal and appropriate. The spiritual trouble comes when we listen to them *all* without deciding which ones are worthy of our time and energy.

We aren't living in days gone by when times were simple and people had an abundance of free time. Few people sit in porch swings and visit with neighbors anymore. Even lazy weekend mornings are rare in our culture. We always have places to go, people to see, and things to do. For that reason, we must *choose* which voices we will listen and respond to. If we are to practice contentment in our lives, we must ignore the voices that would disrupt out intimacy with Jesus. They are not inherently wrong, they are just overwhelming. A wise Christian simply can't be focused on everything that calls out for his or her attention.

Finding Contentment

In a fallen world that revolves around having more, doing more, and being more, how is a believer to find contentment? How do we experience a heartfelt satisfaction with life in a world that promotes dissatisfaction? God has not left us without biblical examples and guidance for finding contentment despite the forces that work against us.

The apostle Paul lived in a turbulent environment hardly conducive to a life of contentment. If contentment came from circumstances, he didn't stand a chance. He said that he had been imprisoned, beaten more times than he could count, and threatened by death. He had been stoned, stranded out in the middle of the ocean for a day and night, and deprived of sleep and food. He had slept outside, exposed to cold weather (2 Corinthians 11:23-27).

In view of these things, Paul made a striking statement in Philippians 4:11 where he said, "I have learned to be content in whatever circumstances I am." How could he learn to be content, considering the kind of life he experienced?

He *learned*. What lesson taught him that?

"Even if I am executed here and now, I'll rejoice…join me in my rejoicing. Whatever you do, don't feel sorry for me" (Philippians 2:17 THE MESSAGE). How could Paul write those words from prison? In Philippians 3:1, he wrote, "Finally, my brethren, rejoice in the Lord. To write the same thing again is no trouble to me, and it is a safeguard for you." Then again, he wrote, "Rejoice in the Lord always; again I will say, rejoice!" (4:4). These were the words of a man who thought he was on death row!

Another servant of Christ is also a worthy example of contentment. Despite the fact that he suffered for his faith, the apostle John showed remarkable contentment. Exiled on the island of Patmos because of his ministry and alone with his Divine Lover, he received a revelation of Jesus Christ that reaches to the end of time. Early in the revelation he received, John saw something that sustained him and brought him contentment in his exile.

What were the lessons Paul and John learned from the Divine Lover that enabled them to confidently and calmly live their lives in contentment? John gives insight into the matter by describing what he saw in Revelation 4:1-2:

> After these things I looked, and behold, *a door standing open* in heaven, and the first voice which I had heard, like the sound of a trumpet speaking with me, said, "Come up here, and I will show you what must take place after these things." Immediately I was in the Spirit; and behold, *a throne was standing in heaven, and One sitting on the throne* (emphasis added).

The two things John saw at that moment are essential to contentment. Whether a person lived two millennia ago or lives in a metropolitan city today, the roadway to contentment hasn't changed. The path is always through Jesus Christ.

A Supernatural Reality Around Us

The first thing that John saw was a door standing open in heaven.[4] What is the significance of this door? A door is a passageway connecting two different places. In this instance, the passage was between two realms—the natural and the supernatural.

The Holy Spirit called John through this door to see beyond the natural world into the eternal world. His body was on Patmos, but for a time, he was able to see beyond the bounds of his physical location to his spiritual home. John saw that he was actually living in two worlds at the same time—the physical and the spiritual.

As a Christian, you too live in dual worlds. If you are to experience the rhythm of God's grace through contentment in your life, you must look beyond the physical world and recognize another dimension where you also live. Contentment vanishes like dew in the desert sun if the only things we can know are the visible circumstances of our lives. We also live in a reality we cannot see.

The apostle Paul had learned contentment through this same lesson. He wrote in 2 Corinthians 4:18, "We look not at the things which are seen, but at the things which are not seen; for the things which are seen are temporal, but the things which are not seen are eternal."

Paul said the same thing as John: We live in a world we can't see with our eyes.

Which reality do you focus on? If your focus is only on the natural world, you are suffering from shortsightedness. Using the lens of faith, look beyond the temporary world and circumstances and see another world. You won't find the source of contentment in the natural realm. However, a supernatural contentment waits for you in the other world, just beyond the door of faith.

In this dual world—physical and spiritual—the spiritual world is the *dominant* world. Believers find our real home in this dominant world. Our residence in this physical world is only temporary, but our residence in the spiritual world is permanent. This is the foundation for contentment in this life. When the outlook is bleak, try the upward look! You are, at this very moment, with God in Christ Jesus.

The enemy of our souls robs us of contentment when he causes us to look away from eternity and become fixated on the temporal circumstances of this life. One example of this is found in the Old Testament in 2 Kings 6:8-17. Eugene Peterson recounts the story well in *The Message:*

> One time when the king of Aram was at war with Israel, after consulting with his officers, he said, "At such and such a place I want an ambush set."
>
> The Holy Man sent a message to the king of Israel: "Watch out when you're passing this place, because Aram has set an ambush there."

So the king of Israel sent word concerning the place of which the Holy Man had warned him.

This kind of thing happened all the time.

The king of Aram was furious over all this. He called his officers together and said, "Tell me, who is leaking information to the king of Israel? Who is the spy in our ranks?"

But one of his men said, "No, my master, dear king. It's not any of us. It's Elisha the prophet in Israel. He tells the king of Israel everything you say, even when you whisper it in your bedroom."

The king said, "Go and find out where he is. I'll send someone and capture him."

The report came back, "He's in Dothan."

Then he dispatched horses and chariots, an impressive fighting force. They came by night and surrounded the city.

Early in the morning a servant of the Holy Man got up and went out. Surprise! Horses and chariots surrounding the city! The young man exclaimed, "Oh, master! What shall we do?"

He said, "Don't worry about it—there are more on our side than on their side."

Then Elisha prayed, "O God, open his eyes and let him see."

The eyes of the young man were opened and he saw. A wonder! The whole mountainside full of horses and chariots of fire surrounding Elisha!

This story is a perfect example of the connection between our focus and contentment. When the servant of Elisha could see only the physical world, panic struck him and contentment disappeared instantly. Elisha, however, wasn't focused on the temporal but looked through the door into the eternal, where everything was under control.

You are no different. Your life is hidden with Christ in God. Your roots are in heaven even as you read this. Your contentment comes from that life, not this one. Don't look for contentment from the temporal things of this world. Contentment is your birthright as a believer, but experiencing it is a spiritual discipline, learned as you look beyond what you can see in the natural world and, by faith, see the truth as it exists in the supernatural world.

A Sovereign Ruler over Us

As John received this revelation he looked through the door and saw a throne. The throne reminds us that the King is in charge. The events of your life aren't unfolding by random chance. The Psalmist wrote, "And in Your book were all written the days that were ordained for me, when as yet there was not one of them" (Psalm 139:16).

A sovereign God has written the script for the drama of life. The world is not hanging in the balance with the outcome yet to be determined. Some people seem to believe that the throngs of heaven are on one side of the stadium and the demons of hell are on the other, each hoping their side wins. In this scenario, man's decisions will determine who wins. Meanwhile, God is keeping His fingers crossed. With that perspective, we should not be surprised that so few experience contentment!

That religious humanism is an insult to God's sovereignty. It puts man in the driver's seat and makes God nothing more than a nervous passenger who is doing all He can do to make sure everything turns out all right. It's a perspective that portrays God as sometimes encouraging us, sometimes threatening us, but always hoping that man will respond in the right way.

Believe me, all of heaven isn't holding its breath waiting to see how things turn out in the end. We aren't at the bottom of the ninth with the bases loaded and the enemy's home-run slugger up to bat. The fact is that eternity's headlines have already been written. They read, "God Wins!"

When John saw the throne, Someone was *sitting* on it. Sitting—not standing (see also 1 Kings 22:19; Isaiah 6:1; Daniel 7:9). Your heavenly Father isn't pacing the corridors of heaven, worrying about how things will be resolved. He's seated because He already has everything worked out to the last detail. He is omniscient—nothing takes Him by surprise. He already knows everything. No variables are unknown to Him. God doesn't *react*. He only acts.

If His omniscience gives Him knowledge of everything, His omnipotence means He has the power to do His will. God is all-powerful. The Bible teaches that He will do whatever He wants, and no person or thing can stop Him (Daniel 4:35). Why He sometimes allows things that seem wrong to us and doesn't allow things that seem right is a mystery. It doesn't sit well with our human ego, but God is all-wise, and His job is to be in charge. Ours is to trust. That's the only way we will ever be content in life.

Either God is in control of everything that happens or we can't be sure He is in charge of anything. Sometimes when evil things happen in this world, some well-meaning Christians will argue, "God had nothing to with that!"

Is that so?

Did He know about it in advance?

Did He allow it?

Could He have stopped it?

The obvious answer is yes. God is connected to and stands in authority over *everything*. Anything outside the realm of His control would be as great as He is, and nothing is as great as God.

If you can think of incidents that you believe God could not have prevented, then a horrifying question must be considered. What *else* might happen that's beyond God's control? If God can't prevent some things from happening, if some things are beyond His will and control, then maybe the worst is yet to come! We would have no reason to expect a trace of contentment in life if a single thing can happen apart from God's control.

Thankfully, the truth is that *nothing* can happen independent of His authority.

Why, then, does God allow events that seem terrible to us? Only in heaven will we learn the answer to some questions. In the meantime, we need to be sure that we don't base our understanding of God on our circumstances. To the contrary, we must interpret our circumstances according to who God is and what we do understand about Him. We know at least one thing about God—He is love (1 John 4:8).

Don't try to understand God by your circumstances. Look at your circumstances through the grid of God's love, and like Paul, learn to be content in any circumstance. You can be content because the victory has already been won for every battle you'll ever face.

Do we really believe these words?

> Through many dangers, toils, and snares, I have already come.
> 'Tis grace that brought me safe thus far, and grace will lead me home.

Eternity is called *home* because we already live there. In some way that our human minds cannot grasp, you and I are actually already seated with Christ beside the throne of God. The apostle Paul wrote:

> But God, being rich in mercy, because of His great love with which He loved us, even when we were dead in our transgressions, made us alive together with Christ (by grace you have been saved), and raised us up with Him, and

seated us with Him in the heavenly places in
Christ Jesus (Ephesians 2:4-6).

Harry Ironside, a great preacher of the early twentieth
century, once had preached on this passage just before
he greeted a young child after the service.

"Did you enjoy the message?" Ironside asked the little
boy.

"Yes, sir," the child answered.

"What did you understand from my sermon?" Ironside
asked.

"Well," answered the boy, "I didn't understand it all,
but I learned one thing. We're sittin' pretty, ain't we?"

That's a good reason for contentment—in Jesus Christ,
"we're sittin' pretty."

The rhythm of contentment can permeate every aspect
of our existence. If the old spiritual song is true that says,
"This world is not my home. I'm just passing through,"
then why seek contentment from this brief stopover? Look
through the open door and recognize that your Divine
Lover is sitting on a throne, ensuring that everything is
unfolding according to plan.

LOOKING UPWARD

1. List the ways you have tried to find happiness in
   your life.

   On a scale of 1 to 10, rate each item's effective-
   ness in bringing you happiness. Did any items on
   your list bring you only temporary happiness?

   Many Christians are happy. However, the New
   Testament associates happiness with something
   external. If you are happy, thank God for it.
   However, realize that believers all over the world

have a deep, abiding joy, but all don't have happiness.

I have spoken to Christians in a leper colony in India. I have met with preachers in China who were literally running for their lives, trying to stay a step ahead of the authorities. Families in some places have seen their loved ones martyred. These precious believers are as far removed from happiness as one can be, yet they have joy and contentment.

In your notebook, explain the difference between happiness and joy. Describe times when you have experienced joy without happiness. Have you ever experienced happiness without joy? Ask the Holy Spirit to deepen your understanding of the difference between the two and enable you to never settle for happiness alone.

2. In what ways has contemporary culture's definition of success influenced you?

How do you define success? Do you consider yourself to be successful? What would have to happen in your life for you to be satisfied with your level of success? Write a description of what your life would have to look like before you could honestly say, "That's enough. I don't need any more in life." Has your desire for success affected your relationship with Jesus Christ in any way? Your answers will reveal much about your perspective on success. Success is not bad, but when the goal to be successful becomes the consuming element of our lives, contentment will become impossible. How strong is your drive to succeed?

3. List the top ten things that consume your time.

Pray about each one of the items on your list. Lay them out before the Divine Lover. Can He express

His life through you in each of these areas? Does the list need to be shortened?

The items on this list are the things to which you give your allegiance. Are they worthy of that allegiance? When you leave this physical world, will you be confident that you have invested your lifetime wisely? Ask the Holy Spirit to show you if other things should be added to this list or if He wants you to remove any.

4. What is the most challenging circumstance in your life right now?

In your notebook, write a description of the circumstance and describe it's affect on you. Do you interpret the circumstance by what you can see in this world, or are you looking through the open doorway into the spiritual world?

Slowly read 2 Kings 6:8-17 again and ask the Holy Spirit to help you personalize it. Are you more like Elisha or the servant? Pray that your eyes will be opened.

Dear Father,

I know that You alone can satisfy my heart. Teach me to find complete fulfillment in you. May I embrace Your joy as the source of contentment. Thank You for the times I am happy. At times of unhappiness, may I look beyond the door and see You on Your throne and find contentment in knowing that You have everything under control. Amen.

Part Two
The Inward Look

4

Contemplation: Idleness with the Almighty

HERMAN MELVILLE'S *MOBY DICK* INCLUDES an intense scene in which Captain Ahab's whaling boat presses through a churning sea in pursuit of the great white whale, Moby Dick. One can almost smell the salt air and feel the ocean spray as Melville describes the chase. The sailors are conscious of nothing but the pounding waves, the violent winds, and the great sea monster beneath the water.

Bulging muscles are taut, and determined minds are irrevocably resolved to do whatever is necessary to triumph in this cosmic battle between good and evil. The swells of the ocean waves lift the whaleboat high above the water's surface, only to slam it back down again. But the morally outraged Captain Ahab will not give up. Everything that matters is in the balance at this moment. No energy or determination can be spared. The boat may break apart, but to forfeit the fight is out of the question. The demon beneath must be destroyed. As Eugene Peterson notes:

In this boat, however, there is one man
who does nothing. He doesn't hold an oar; he
doesn't perspire; he doesn't shout. He is languid
in the crash and cursing. This man is the har-
pooner, quiet and poised, waiting. And then this
sentence: "To ensure the greatest efficiency in
the dart, the harpooners of this world must start
to their feet out of idleness, and not out of toil."[1]

Nobody would dispute that a cosmic battle exists today
between the forces of good and evil. We see this struggle
on the sea of humanity in every culture of the world.
Pastors and churches urge us to not give up the ship but
labor on, to fight at all costs to ensure victory. Recruiters
appeal to our sense of what is moral and right to enlist
us in the struggle.

Every Sunday, sincere Christians rededicate themselves
with a renewed determination to become more involved
and consistent in the battle against evil. Their hearts are
in the right place. They feel the need to do something,
but where can they be most effective in the boat?

The majority are determined to become better oarsmen
who will work harder. A few are sure they sense the calling of Captain Ahab on their lives. They express their intent
to attend a religious naval academy where they can learn
to be the skipper of their own boat. They want to lead
other sailors and together conquer the demon of the
depths.

Nothing is wrong in this scenario, but something is *missing*. Where are the harpooners of the twenty-first-century
church? How are we supposed to overcome the demons
of the depths? In many instances, we don't even know
how to strike a death blow against the carnality of our
own behavior, much less admonish others about theirs or
lead others like ourselves into battle. Note Melville's statement again: "To ensure the greatest efficiency in the dart,

the harpooners of this world must start to their feet out of idleness, and not out of toil."

Idleness? When a violent storm is raging, when our enemy is so close that our very lives are in danger, when everybody else around us is frantic with hyperactivity, idleness is not a natural response. Yet surely God has called each of us to an idleness of sorts. For the person who wants to know triumph in the struggle, this idleness is indispensable. Those who are weary with fatigue are in no condition to strike the fatal blow against the enemy. In idleness we find our strength. We will now consider the spiritual discipline of contemplation—idleness with God.

The Inner Man

In Part 1 of *The Godward Gaze* we examined spiritual disciplines that help us look upward into the lovely face of our Father. We discussed lifting our hearts upward to Him through awareness, quietness, and contentment. Each of these rhythms of grace can become a bridge to deeper intimacy with Christ.

Other spiritual disciplines prompt us to look not *upward* but *inward*. These disciplines draw us toward the sacred center of ourselves, where Christ dwells within us. They enable us not only to know Him more intimately but also to know ourselves better. They are the pillars that support our interior life. These inward disciplines are contemplative prayer, biblical meditation, and identification with Christ.

What is our interior life? To those who are unfamiliar with the spiritual disciplines, the term can sound too mystical or self-oriented. But God intends for us to live our lives from the inside out. Our strength ultimately depends on the resilience of this interior part of ourselves. This is the hidden you, that part that nobody except God sees. It's what is left when everything superficial is taken away. It isn't what you do or what other people think about you. It's the you that lives behind your reputation and accomplishments, the you that, although often obscured, actually drives your attitudes and actions.

The apostle Paul prayed that the Ephesian church would "be strengthened with power through His Spirit in the inner man" (Ephesians 3:16). He understood that life is lived from within. As God strengthens us through His Spirit in the inner man, we experience the ministry of the Spirit of Christ within us—and live moment by moment in recognition that He alone is our source of life.

The indwelling Christ will transform us from the inside. And yet so often we get the process backward. Legalistic religion would reform us from the outside, stressing that we can change simply by behaving in certain ways. The effect of legalism is always the same. Jesus said we may clean up well on the outside, but on the inside we can still be full of filth (Matthew 23:27-28).

The Holy Spirit doesn't simply *reform* believers. He *transforms* us so that we are "filled up to all the fullness of God" (Ephesians 3:19). Because you are a believer, Christ lives inside your spirit at this very moment. His intent is to express His life through your total being—spirit (inner being), soul (mind, emotions, and will) and body (actions).

Idle Time with Jesus Christ

How does Christ bring about this transformation? One way is through intimate interaction, which you can share with Him through *contemplative prayer*. Earlier we referred to this as "idleness" with God.

Most of us didn't grow up with an understanding of contemplative prayer. We learned to pray, but prayer gradually became a legalistic discipline instead of a natural rhythm of grace. Eventually, some of us found ourselves praying in much the same way we brush our teeth. Prayer was a good habit we developed because good Christians *should* pray. But such prayer probably brought us very little fulfillment and intimacy with our Father.

Oh, we were earnest in our prayers. But mostly prayer was a sincere intellectual practice with no resulting inward transformation. But God's desire is that our prayer life should be enriching and sometimes even *enthralling*. When was the last time you enjoyed an enthralling, transforming prayer session?

If you pray because of obligation, guilt, or legalism, you are unlikely to have been enthralled anytime recently. By contrast, contemplative prayer and all of the other spiritual disciplines flow from a river of pure grace. Nothing so quickly kills our faith faster than legalism.

How can you know whether your prayer life is polluted with legalism? Consider these legalistic misunderstandings about prayer.

Praying for a Certain Amount of Time

Many believers have been taught that the best way to have an effective prayer life is to set aside a certain number of minutes every day for prayer. They think that if they log in for the set amount of time each day, they are on track. If they miss that time or even cut it short, they feel guilty and wonder if God is displeased.

Setting time aside for prayer may be helpful, but simply being alone and saying prayers for a certain amount of time does not make us virtuous. God doesn't check our prayer card every day to see if we have logged enough time on His time clock.

The scribes in Jesus' day were renowned for praying long prayers (Mark 12:38-40), but Jesus said they would receive greater condemnation than others in the end. A person's frequency or length of time in prayer is not what constitutes an effective prayer life. This isn't to suggest that what happens during time spent in prayer has no value or that time isn't necessary, but time *alone* has no intrinsic value in prayer. What goes on during that time is what makes the difference.

Saying the Right Things

Many people tend to want formulas for their relationship to God. We have learned innumerable methods for prayer. Some people repeatedly recite short, memorized prayers. Others move through a long series of steps starting with adoration and ending with petition. We have received a plethora of prayer patterns.

What is prayer? The many formulas offered in the contemporary church may leave us wondering, Did God mean for prayer to be *that* complicated? We should not expect to find some magic method for communicating with the God who knows our very heart. Imagine a marriage where partners learn a step-by-step program for talking to each other. Every day they discipline themselves to cover all the communication bases so that they speak the right words. What level of intimacy would exist in that marriage?

Two men once prayed as they stood in church. The first prayed a pious prayer, pointing out his impressive track record of religious service. The other prayed a pitiful prayer, simply begging, "God! Have mercy on me!" Jesus said God heard and answered the second one's prayers (Luke 18:13-14). Apparently God looks beyond words and right into the heart when someone prays.

Are Words Always Necessary?

This is another common error that many people believe. God intends prayer to be a dialogue, not a monologue. True prayer is a two-way communication of love between two people who care deeply for each other. The Divine Lover wants communication in ways that sometimes transcend words.

Husbands and wives often express their love most deeply through sexual intimacy. In a heightened state of exhilaration with each other, caught up in the emotional and physical ecstasy of the sacred oneness of a marriage ordained by God, two people experience a level of communion beyond words.

When we are in the grasp of pure love's intensity, words aren't always necessary. The sacred love of man and wife can't be reduced to words at that moment. They share a subliminal communion that is more profound than words could ever express. Married partners who share love in a God-ordained and God-blessed way sometimes don't need to say anything. Both partners just *know.*

This analogy is not irreverent in any way. God Himself chose the metaphor of becoming one flesh in marriage to teach us about the relationship between Christ and His church (Ephesians 5:31-32). The Song of Solomon is a graphic depiction of physical intimacy. Bible scholars are generally in agreement that the book is intended to communicate the intimate aspects of God's relationship to those He loves.

If you want to see your prayer life come alive, allow the Divine Lover to transform your thoughts so that you begin to see it not as your duty but as an opportunity for you and God to share your love in a sacred and intimate way that will sometimes go beyond spoken words. Prayer will certainly include words, but not every time or all the time.

If your concept of prayer includes saying the right words every day for the right amount of time, your prayer life is probably a discipline in the most negative sense of the word. However, when we come to understand what praying in grace means, we discover that the discipline of prayer is like physical intimacy. It isn't effortless, but it certainly couldn't be considered a mere duty. It is a natural rhythm of grace operating in the life of one who is in love with Jesus Christ.

Praying in Grace

What does *praying in grace* mean? If you think of prayer only as an orchestrated event that must include certain religious elements in order to be valid, the Holy Spirit may need to renew your mind on the subject. Would you be willing to temporarily suspend any preconceived ideas you may have about the meaning of prayer and be open to an expanded perspective? Consider the following characteristics of grace-based prayer.

Knowing That He Completely Loves Us

The Bible teaches that the essence of God's nature is love (1 John 4:8). If prayer is indeed communication between the believer and God, why would our Father desire to commune with us in a way that contradicts His very nature? How do you think God sees you when you pray? He can only relate to you in love. He *is* love personified, so because of His very essence, He relates to those for whom He gave His life in loving interaction.

To think that God is frowning at you when you pray is a terrible and binding error. *He is not.* God *loves* you, and nothing you have done or ever could do is going to change His mind about you. His loving thoughts are always toward you. Theologian Angelus Silesius astutely observed in the fifteenth century, "If God stopped thinking of me, He would cease to exist." God's nature is to continuously think of you, and His thoughts are always loving.

Reveling in the Love of God

Consider this story. A peasant stopped by his village church every day after work on his way home. He set his pickax and spade outside and entered the church, where he sat in silence for about an hour. Then he stood, left the church, and continued on his way home.

The village priest watched this man from the back of the church. Nothing in the old man's actions explained why he was there or what was in his heart. Puzzled by the strange habit, the priest decided to approach the man and ask about his practice.

"Why do you come into my church day after day, old man?" the priest asked. "And why do you waste your time doing nothing when you are here?"

The old man looked at him.

"Father," he said humbly, "I simply look at Him and He looks at me, and we tell each other that we love each other."[2]

This old story demonstrates the true meaning of contemplative prayer. It doesn't require having a quiet time for a set amount of time or saying the right words so that God springs into action on our behalf. Contemplative prayer is founded on love.

Contemplation has been defined as "the gaze of the soul upon God." Some have called it "the prayer of loving attentiveness," or the "prayer of loving regard." This spiritual discipline is essentially about loving God and allowing Him to love us.[3] To contemplate something means to set our full, undivided attention upon it.

Contemplation is not an attempt to understand something. Contemplation isn't the same as meditation, in which we *think.* Instead, in contemplation, we *look.* We *listen.* We set our focus on the beauty of Jesus Christ and simply spend idle time with Him, allowing Him to set the agenda for our time together. To the obsessively driven doers of the world this may seem like a waste of time, but experience will prove that time "wasted" with Jesus is time well spent.

Henri Nouwen notes:

> Prayer is primarily a useless hour...Prayer is primarily to do nothing in the presence of God. It is to be not useful and to remind myself that

if anything important in life happens, it is God who does it. So when I go into the day, I go with the conviction that God is the one who brings fruits to my work, and I do not have to act as though I am in control of things.[4]

To be idle with Jesus Christ in contemplative prayer is to bask in His warm embrace. It's to simply be still and know that He is God (Psalm 46:10). The word *idleness* strikes a raw nerve for many people. In our highly scheduled culture, the concept seems to suggest a lazy passivity. "What are we to *do* in contemplative prayer?" contemporary, hyperactive Christians may ask. Nouwen responds:

> The first answer is nothing. Just be present to the One who wants your attention and listen! It is precisely in this "useless" presence to God that we can gradually die to our illusions of power and control and give ear to the voice of love hidden in the center of our being. But "doing nothing, being useless" is not as passive as it sounds. In fact it requires effort and great attentiveness. It calls us to an active listening in which we make ourselves available to God's healing presence and can be made new.[5]

Listening to the Voice of the Divine Lover

Do you hear Jesus Christ speak to you? Some cynical critics say, "I worry about these people who say God talks to them." However, Jesus Christ wasn't at all ambiguous about this matter. He said, "My sheep hear my voice, and I know them, and they follow me" (John 10:27). The Bible is clear about it—the Lover of our souls wants us to hear Him.

In the play *The Search for Signs of Intelligent Life in the Universe,* Lily Tomlin's character asks, "Why is it that when we speak to God we are said to be praying, but when

God speaks to us we are said to be schizophrenic?"[6] A cursory reading of the New Testament proves that early Christians considered hearing the voice of God a common experience. In the years that have transpired, the Divine Lover has not become mute.

Contemplative prayer involves waiting before the Lord with anticipation that He will express His love to you in clear, understandable ways. Soren Kierkegaard once observed, "A man prayed, and at first he thought that prayer was talking. But then he became more and more quiet until in the end he realized that prayer is listening."

Some Christians think that God can only speak in austere, majestic terms. Maybe He would even speak in King James English. This misunderstanding of how God speaks can keep them from hearing His voice.

In his book, *Without Feathers,* Woody Allen offers an essay that spoofs the biblical story of Abraham and Isaac. As Allen tells the story, Abraham is reporting to Sarah and Isaac about God's instructions for him to offer Isaac as a sacrifice. This description contains elements of humor, but it isn't so far removed from the way some Christians think that God must speak to them.

> And Abraham awoke in the middle of the night and said to his only son, Isaac, "I have had a dream where the voice of the Lord sayeth that I must sacrifice my only son, so put your pants on." And Isaac trembled and said, "So what did you say? I mean when He brought this whole thing up?" "What am I going to say?" Abraham said. "I'm standing there at two A.M. in my underwear with the Creator of the Universe. Should I argue?" "Well, did he say why he wants me sacrificed?" Isaac asked his father. But Abraham said, "The faithful do not question. Now let's go because I have a heavy day tomorrow." And Sarah...said, "How doth thou

know it was the Lord?"...And Abraham answered, "Because I know it was the Lord. It was a deep, resonant voice, well modulated, and nobody in the desert can get a rumble in it like that."[7]

We must learn to recognize the Divine Lover's voice. Don't wait for a deep, resonant, well-modulated sound. The Lord may express His love to you in unexpected ways and at unexpected times. Contemplative prayer trains us to hear His voice and recognize who we are hearing.

My friend Bill told me about an experience he shared with Jesus one morning several hours before dawn. His work schedule had been particularly busy. Consequently, He had seen little of his children lately.

On this particular day, he had to leave the house long before his wife and children awoke. Just before he left, he quietly slipped into the bedroom where his son lay sleeping. Standing beside his bed, he watched him by the dim light.

Suddenly Bill was overwhelmed with love for his son. Emotion rose up within him as he admired this child whom he loves so very much. At that moment, Bill heard the voice of his heavenly Father speak to him. *Bill,* the Lord said, *Do you know how many times I have done this exact thing with you as you slept?*

Bill said, "Until He told me, I had never thought about my heavenly Father watching me sleep!" That morning, a renewed young dad left his house, wiping tears of joy from his eyes. Quietly he gave thanks for the love shared between two fathers and their sons.

Do you want to gaze into the loving face of your Father through the lens of contemplation? The suggestions that follow may help you in your Godward gaze. Don't twist these suggestions into a formula for contemplative prayer. Some may fit your personality; others may not. Utilize those that work for you and ask the Holy Spirit to show you other specific ways to practice the art of contemplation.

Look within yourself to the indwelling Christ. You don't have to reach far away to find Jesus. Instead, look inward where He is patiently waiting, longing for the two of you to stare deeply into each other's eyes and express a greater love than the world can ever know.

LOOKING UPWARD

1. Write a short description of your prayer life.

Ask the Holy Spirit to show you whether your prayer life is based on legalism or grace. Pray right now and ask, *Lord, teach me to pray.*

2. Sit quietly and focus your attention on Jesus Christ.

Resist the impulse to immediately begin using words for prayer. Set your mind on the love that your heavenly Father has for you. Reject analytical thoughts about what this time is supposed to accomplish. You don't have to accomplish anything. Just turn your heart toward Him in quiet submission and wait.

If you seem to experience nothing, don't become discouraged. If your thoughts tend to wander, remember that this is completely normal for people who have seldom known a quiet moment within themselves throughout their lifetime. Gently bring your focus back to Jesus Christ.

3. Listen to the gentle prompting of the Holy Spirit.

You have no agenda for your time of contemplative prayer other than to set your attention on Him. But God's Spirit may gently guide your thoughts into various areas of your life where He wants to act. He may cause you to pray for yourself or others using words. However, you will not always have to frame your requests in words.

Sometimes you may simply recognize a need, lift it upward, and lay it at the feet of Jesus without a word. If you don't know what to say, say nothing. Simply present your requests to Him by imagining that you are laying them out before Him.

4. Use sanctified imagination to enjoy the affection of the divine lover.

The emphasis of the New Age Movement on visualization has caused many Christians to be afraid of using their imaginations at all in their relationship to God. However, the believer's imagination is a powerful tool for experiencing intimacy with Him. Tragically, many believers are convinced the imagination is the enemy's domain. If the enemy of our souls will readily use our imagination, we should yield it to the Holy Spirit for God's glory. Don't allow others' mistakes to rob you of the benefits of your imagination.

Some Christians imagine their heavenly Father embracing them with a big hug. Others imagine themselves sitting on His lap like a child. Still others imagine Him lovingly gazing into their eyes. Ask the Holy Spirit to teach you how to combine your imagination with biblical faith to experience a deeper sense of intimacy with God.

Try this simple exercise. As you read these next few paragraphs, slow down your thought process. Don't rush through these lines as though you were in a hurry to accomplish a mission. Use your imagination and *see* by faith what is described in the paragraphs that follow.

Imagine Jesus walking into the room where you are right now. He walks across the room and stands directly in front of you. He reaches out, puts His arms around you, and pulls you close to Himself to hug you.

Relax.

Still your busy mind.

Just rest in His embrace.

He gently presses His face against your own and quietly whispers in your ear, "I love you *so* much. Do you know how proud I am of you? I love you more than you can possibly know. Sh-h-h. Be still and know that I love you."

Listen to Him.

Wait until you sense an inner calmness.

Ask Him to speak a personal word, just to you.

Listen.

Do you hear His voice?

Linger here, in this still, quiet place, and allow Him to express His love.

Wait until the appropriate time to resume normal activity.

Revel in His love.

Don't rush...stay awhile longer.

Are you uncomfortable with this exercise? Is anything I've described unbiblical? Is anything untrue about the above scenario? Jesus *does* love you just as I have described. He *does* embrace you in His arms and long to express His love to you in meaningful ways. Don't *pretend*. By faith, see in your mind's eye something that is real.

Don't be uncomfortable with such intimacy. Sometimes men protest that such an exercise feels unnatural to them. They are correct. It is unnatural. It's *supernatural.*

Relax. This isn't an issue about gender. Learn to appreciate your loving Father's embrace the way you enjoyed feeling your earthly father's arms around you when you were a child. Despite the messages of contemporary culture, men don't outgrow the need for affection. If you are uncomfortable, practice the awareness of His affectionate presence until you are comfortable.

If you don't see yourself as an affectionate person by nature, ask the Holy Spirit to help you see that your heavenly Father *is* an affectionate Person. He wants to pour out His affection on you. Once you have learned to receive it from Him, you will be encouraged to discover how much more easily you can share your affection with others.

Contemplative prayer is simply becoming idle with Jesus Christ and reveling in His tender love. From that idleness we are able to move into action, energized by a divine power known only by the "harpooners of heaven." From that idleness we will discover how to perform our activities in the awareness of a supernatural love. Learn to be idle with the one who passionately declares His love for us.

Dear Father,

I want to be transformed in the inner man by continuous communion with You. Set me free from the busyness of other things so that I can have idle time with You. Teach me how to sit calmly in Your presence so that I might find healing and peace as You declare Your love for me. I want to learn to contemplate You and Your love for me. Amen.

5

Meditation:
Bathing in His Word

SOME PEOPLE BELIEVE EVERYTHING THEY HEAR. Advertisers spend millions of dollars every year because TV viewers watch infomercials and believe what paid actors tell them. Wide-eyed enthusiasts hawk creams, pills, oils, machines, and gadgets with their "unsolicited testimonials."

Almost rabid with excitement, they preach the gospel of a glorified body—not in heaven but right here and now—all for three low monthly payments (shipping and handling not included). To hear them talk, these items have changed their lives. Buy them all and you can have thicker hair, whiter teeth, stronger nails, a flatter stomach, younger skin, bulging biceps, and anything else that would require you to hire a bodyguard to keep the hands of the opposite sex off you. The only requirement on your part is to *act now!*

Given the chance, most of us would change something about ourselves if we could. Our appearance, our personality, our emotional makeup—we wish God had done something differently when He assembled us. And so our desire for change prompts us to watch those infomercials, to test those promises, to find that one *something* out there that can make a great difference in our lives.

In fact, something *can* make a difference. Unsolicited testimonials throughout history have attested to its transforming power. Those who gave these testimonies weren't paid for them either. In fact, some were killed for giving them.

What is this all-purpose transformer that can change your life?

You probably already have it at home.

It's your Bible. The Bible's power to transform human lives is too great to be measured. Some people will believe testimonies of strangers who affirm they've been helped by this year's newest trinket, but they don't take seriously the witness of a parade of people throughout history who have unanimously testified to the power of God's Word to transform their lives.

Almost every home in the Western world has at least one Bible. Sometimes you'll see one on the dashboard of somebody's car, left there since church last Sunday. You'll also find one in the top drawer of the nightstand in your hotel room. Or you might see a large ornate family Bible, placed ever-so-tidily as a decoration on the coffee table. If you browse through the shelves of books in your local thrift store, you'll likely see lots of discarded Bibles— leather Bibles, hardbacks, paperbacks—in just about every version. Bibles are everywhere in America.

How about *your* Bible? Where is it right now? How do you use it? Do you recognize the power of the Bible to transform your life if you use it in the way God intends? Have you fully grasped the value of the treasure you hold in your hands every time you pick up your Bible?

I'll never forget an elderly lady I met in China. She was probably in her early eighties and had a radiant smile. As we visited with her, I gave her several hundred dollars that I had been asked to deliver as a gift. She smiled and graciously said, "Thank you."

Then I pulled three Bibles out of my bag that I had smuggled into the country. When I handed them to her, she began to cry with joy.

"I appreciate this," she said, holding up the envelope with the money, "but I *love* this!" she said, holding up the Bibles. In China, Christians still copy the Bible by hand and circulate it in the underground church. That saint knew what she had in her hand.

Listen to the testimonials of a few people whose lives have been transformed by God's Word.

- King David: "[His] word is a lamp to my feet and a light to my path."

- The apostle Paul: "All Scripture is inspired by God and is profitable..."

- Abraham Lincoln: "I believe the Bible is the best gift God has ever given to man. All the good from the Savior of the world is communicated to us through this book."

- Napolean Bonaparte: "The Bible is no mere book, but it's a living creature with a power that conquers all who oppose it."

- Dwight L. Moody: "I know the Bible is inspired because it inspires me."

- Charles Haddon Spurgeon: "Nobody ever outgrows Scripture; the Book widens and deepens with our years."

What *is* the Bible? Is it simply a compilation of religious writings from centuries ago? As a Christian, you know better. The Bible is God's divinely inspired, written Word for man. It claims to be "living and active and sharper than any two-edged sword…and able to judge the thoughts and intentions of the heart" (Hebrews 4:12).

Throughout church history, people have discovered that when they read the Bible with a proper attitude, *it reads them*. If you sincerely look into the Bible, you will discover it looking deep into you. The Bible will diagnose problems you didn't even know you had and then offer a remedy for those problems.

The Word of God is

- pure (Proverbs 30:5 KJV)

- eternal (Isaiah 40:8, 1 Peter 1:23)

- a giver of joy (Jeremiah 15:16)

- a source of faith (Romans 10:17)

- food for the spiritually hungry (Matthew 4:4)

- a spiritual weapon (Ephesians 6:17)

The Bible is not simply *a* book, but *the* Book of all the ages.

What are we to do with this Book that God has entrusted to us and that many have given their lives to preserve? We may approach the Bible in several ways. Each is important in reaping the benefit that God has for us in His Word.

Reading the Bible

Most people simply read the Bible. Reading God's Word can either be a meaningless ritual or an enriching experience, depending on our attitude as we approach it.

One day, after many years of a hedonistic lifestyle, Augustine heard a voice speak to him. The voice said, "Take it and read. Take it and read." Convinced that he was hearing the voice of God, Augustine found a Bible and began to read from Paul's epistle to the Romans.

After a while, Augustine discovered that God's Word arrested him. Later, he would write in his *Confessions,* "I had no wish to read further; there was no need to...it was as though my heart were filled with a light of confidence and all the shadows of my doubt were swept away."[1]

The contributions of St. Augustine to the kingdom of God started when he read from the Bible and discovered that it also read him. If you read the Bible because your heart hungers to meet the Divine Lover there, He will speak to you too. His words always have life-transforming power in them.

Studying the Bible

Some people go a step further in their approach to Scripture. They actually *study* the Bible. Through the Internet, the range of resources for Bible study is unlimited. Additionally, we have never had more books in print designed to help study God's Word. The opportunity for personal benefit from Bible study has never been greater than it is today.

We can use many different methods of Bible study to gain insight into the Scriptures. One way is to *exegete* Scripture—to dissect it, examining each part of a verse. This may include word studies in the original languages to find not only the meaning of words but also the connotation associated with those words in ancient times. Exegesis often involves an examination of the cultural and historical setting within which the text was written.

A more simple method of Bible study is to apply the five W's and an H that Rudyard Kipling wrote about:

> I keep six honest serving men,
> They taught me all I knew,
> Their names are What and Why and When,
> And How and Where and Who.

All Christians, no matter how interested or uninterested they are in in-depth Bible study, should have a few of the basic tools by which they can get more familiar with their Bibles. At a minimum, we all need to have a good Bible dictionary, a concordance for the version we primarily use, and a good one-volume commentary. These are readily available at your local Christian bookstore or through an online bookseller.

If you've never studied the Bible, you might begin with a short book in the New Testament, such as one of Paul's short epistles. Your pastor may be willing to give you guidance on how to begin a personal study. Kay Arthur, through her Precept Ministries, has produced some remarkable material that has helped many learn the Bible for the first time through inductive study. Other authors have developed good material too. If you've read but have never studied the Bible, you've only skimmed the surface.

Meditating on the Bible

Beyond reading and studying the Bible—fine activities that they are—is the inward spiritual discipline of Bible meditation. Meditation on Scripture is a spiritual discipline that God's people have embraced for many millennia. It's a way to meet the Divine Lover in a private place where He openly professes His love for you through His Word. As you meditate on the truths of Scripture, real transformation can take place in your innermost being.

To meditate on something is simply to fix our undivided attention on it and think about it deeply. It means to consider a matter from one angle and then another. The word is associated with a cow chewing its cud over and over again until it can be fully digested.

Richard Foster describes the difference between meditation and study:

Whereas the study of Scripture centers on exegesis, the meditation of Scripture centers on internalizing and personalizing the passage. The written word becomes a living word addressed to you. This is not a time for technical studies, or analysis, or even the gathering of material to share with others. Set aside all tendencies toward arrogance and with a humble heart receive the word addressed to you.[2]

British author Tony Horsfall explains the meaning of meditation from a negative viewpoint:

Worry is a form of meditation. When we worry about something we continually dwell on that which is negative and unhelpful. We allow our imagination to run wild, thinking of all the bad things that might happen. Anxious thoughts swirl round and round in our minds. When this happens we are meditating, but unhealthily so. What this shows is that we can all meditate. It is not a matter of intelligence or spiritual prowess. We meditate instinctively. What is important, though, is that we meditate on the right things. We can choose what we meditate upon, and it is possible, with discipline and practice, to turn our minds and attention to more uplifting thoughts.[3]

Most of us didn't grow up learning to meditate on Scripture. We may have read it every day and even studied it, but to *meditate?* That may sound too New Agey or have a bit of an Eastern religious flavor to it. Or maybe it sounds like something done by a seriously spiritual group who live in seclusion and eat nothing but rice and water.

But true meditation is a solidly biblical practice (see Genesis 24:63; Joshua 1:8; Psalm 63:6; 77:12; 104:34; 119:148; 1 Timothy 4:15 KJV). Don't be wary of the concept just because you may associate it with false religions or extremism. Meditation is a lens through which we may experience intimacy with Jesus Christ in profound, life-changing ways. It is a way to experience the Bible for what the Divine Lover intends it to be—a love letter, enticing you toward Him.

Some common misunderstandings of the Bible's purpose may interfere with the discipline of meditation. However, we can easily overcome these barriers simply by accepting the truth about the matter. Consider a few misconceptions that can keep you from enjoying the Bible to the fullest.

Is the Bible an Instruction Manual?

Most of us have heard that the Bible is an operation manual, written to teach us how to live. The Bible *will* give Christians guidance on how to live victoriously in this world, but that's not the reason God has given us the Bible.

To suggest that the Bible exists to give information is to miss the heart of Scripture. As a dad, I taught my children many things. I taught them how to budget money, but I hope they don't see me primarily as a financial consultant. I taught them about spiritual things, but I don't think they relate to me as a theologian.

Do you understand the point?

The Bible will teach you about life, but that's not its primary purpose. If you relate to Scripture as an instruction manual, you will no doubt find helpful guidance there. But you will miss the most important reason for opening your Bible. God's Word will likely reach your head but never touch you in the deepest places of your heart.

Is the Bible a Rule Book?

This is another common idea about the purpose of God's Word. Some people believe that God gave us the Bible to draw behavioral boundaries for living. Their desire is to "live by the Bible." They want to make sure that they follow its teaching to the letter of the law.

Nobody would dispute that the Bible clearly delineates what behavior is glorifying to God and what behavior is sinful. However, God didn't give us His Word so that we would be sure to walk a straight line without veering off in either direction. That approach to the Bible will surely lead to defeat in our lives.

To approach the Bible as a book of rules is to embrace legalism. Nobody in the chains of legalism will experience the joy and peace for which they hunger. When we relate to the Bible as a book of religious laws, we will always have an internal sense of condemnation. That's the very nature of the law. Paul plainly called the law a ministry of death and condemnation (2 Corinthians 3:5-7).

If you have thought of the Bible as a rule book, you've probably struggled to consistently read it. After all, who wants to sit down every day and read a list of things they *must* do or *can't* do. Reading the Bible in this way will take all the joy out of it and suffocate spiritual passion in our lives.

Is the Bible a Book of Literature?

College students often study certain passages of Scripture as great pieces of literature. Without question, parts of Scripture reverberate with literary style. Some of the greatest poetry and prose that exist are in the Bible. That isn't surprising because the source of all creative artistic ability is the Divine Lover.

Most Christians don't have such a low view of Scripture that they see it as only a book of literature, but many do seem to approach it that way. Some Christians approach the Bible in the hopes that its words will give them a warm devotional experience. They are satisfied if they can read a passage that simply gives them a good feeling.

Some churches approach the Bible that way. They present the Scripture as if it's purpose is to provide an inspirational thought to brighten our day before we go on our way into the real world. To some, the Bible is nothing much more than a dispenser of warm-fuzzies.

What Is the Purpose of the Bible?

If the Bible isn't primarily an instruction manual, a rule book, or a collection of great literature, why did God give us His Word? Imagine being able to ask Jesus Christ, "What is the main thing that the Bible should accomplish in my life?"

Pause for a moment and imagine that scenario. What do you think He would say?

The good news is that we don't have to imagine. Jesus did have something to say on the benefits we can experience from the Scripture.

The setting for His explanation is described in John 5. Jesus was in Jerusalem during a feast of the Jews. As He entered the city, He came upon a pool of water at a place called Bethesda.

A great crowd of disabled people gathered around the pool every day because of a miracle that had been happening in that place. Every now and then, an angel came down and stirred up the water in the pool. As soon as he did, the first person in the pool was healed of his or her disease.

One man who was there had been paralyzed for 38 years. Obviously, he hadn't been able to get into the pool. When Jesus came along and saw him, He spoke to the man.

> He said to him, "Do you wish to get well?" The sick man answered Him, "Sir, I have no man to put me into the pool when the water is stirred up, but while I'm coming, another steps down before me." Jesus said to him, "Get up, pick up your pallet and walk" (John 5:6-8).

Instantly the man was made well. He got up, picked up his pallet, and went on his way with great enthusiasm. Jesus had completely healed him.

A little while later, some of the religious Jews saw him carrying his pallet and said, "This is the Sabbath! You are not permitted to carry your pallet today!"

"The man who made me well told me to pick it up and go," the healed man answered.

"Who told you that?" they asked him.

But the healed man didn't know His name because Jesus had slipped away.

A little while later the man saw Jesus again in the temple. This time he asked His name. When he saw those same Jews again, he told them that Jesus had healed him.

They went looking for Jesus until they found Him. They began to challenge Him about what He had done. In fact, they came down on Him hard because He had done this on the Sabbath in violation of their interpretation of God's law (John 5:16).

Considering the response of these Jews, how do you think they approached Scripture? Without a doubt, they saw it as a rule book! They pounced on Jesus because He wasn't keeping the rules.

During His response to their accusations, Jesus told them the main purpose of the Scriptures. This was a group who read the Bible—that is, the Old Testament—religiously. They not only read it but even studied it intensely. But Jesus said they were missing the point.

He said to them, "You search the Scriptures because you think that in them you have eternal life; it is these that testify about Me; and you are unwilling to come to Me so that you may have life" (John 5:39-40). Jesus gives us the main reason to search out the Scriptures—to know Him! The Bible is to lead us to Jesus! That is what *He* said is the benefit of interacting with God's Word.

B I - ST   Christ-Centered Bible Study

We look to our Bible not primarily for information, education, or even inspiration. We come to God's Word for a *revelation* of Jesus Christ! He wants us to see Him on every page in Scripture. Augustine rightly said that "the Holy Scriptures are our letters from home."

Think of the Bible as a photo album. In the New Testament, Jesus is clearly seen standing in the front of pictures on every page. In the Old Testament, He stands in the background of the photograph. However, as we prayerfully meditate on His Word, the Holy Spirit reveals Him to us. Then our hearts are thrilled as we respond, *Oh! There you are, Jesus! I knew you were here!* His response will be to laugh with delight and to embrace us in His arms.

What is meditation? It's bathing in the Word of God until we experience a loving, life-altering encounter with Jesus Christ. (Christians can't have any other kind of encounter with Him.) Meditation is soaking in God's Word until we are drenched in the love and presence of Jesus. It's bathing in His tender acceptance until we are healed.

Don't you love soaking in a hot bath when you're physically exhausted? That's what meditation is to the tired soul. Madame Guyon described it as experiencing "the depths of Jesus Christ." The early church fathers called it *otium sanctum*—Holy Leisure.[4]

One poet, enthralled with Him during meditation described it saying,

> Only to sit and think of God,
> Oh what a joy it is!
> To think the thought, to breathe the Name,
> Earth has no higher bliss![5]

The Christian who hungers for his Divine Lover won't settle for an academic approach to the Bible. Reading and studying God's Word are important, but don't stop there! Ask the Holy Spirit to teach you the spiritual discipline of meditation so that this rhythm of grace can bring the music of heaven into your soul.

Are you ready to practice meditation?

The remainder of the chapter will offer some suggestions that you'll find helpful in your journey. Don't try to turn these suggestions into a magic formula. They are simply guidelines that many have found helpful.

Just relax. If you don't find the satisfaction you're hungry for at this point, don't worry. The Holy Spirit has started you on a journey, and He will make sure you reach your destination (Philippians 1:6).

LOOKING UPWARD

1. Ask the Lord to intimately reveal Himself to you through His Word.

    Before you even pick up your Bible, pause and pray. This isn't a test to determine your spirituality. It isn't an assignment that you can pass or fail. You can do *nothing* to generate an encounter with Jesus. We have all experienced reading the Bible and finding no more benefit from it at the moment than if we were reading the daily newspaper.

    Acknowledge to the Lord that this encounter isn't something you expect to make happen. If you tend to be the type of person who always wants to be in control, ask the Holy Spirit to show you how that characteristic may affect your relationship with Him. You aren't in control, He is. He may sit so quietly with you that you can't detect His presence immediately to give you time to learn that lesson.

    What if you read your Bible using a meditative approach and experience absolutely nothing? Will you feel that you have failed? If so, the Lord may be teaching you that *you* aren't in charge of this process. How could you fail at something that isn't your responsibility to begin with? Continue to seek Him in His Word, and you will ultimately *not* be disappointed. That is a personal guarantee from God Himself (Jeremiah 29:13).

2. Ask the Holy Spirit to guide you concerning where you are to read today.

The Holy Spirit isn't likely to immediately lead you to an obscure or difficult passage. Many find the Psalms a good learning ground for meditation. In the New Testament, the gospels or the epistles of Paul are good places to start with this spiritual discipline.

Read from a text that already makes sense to you on the surface. You will see things beneath the surface as you meditate. Practicing this approach to Scripture will probably be easier for you if you aren't having to try to understand a challenging text. Meditating on that kind of passage certainly has its place, but it usually comes after *study* of the text.

3. Begin to read the Bible very slowly.

When we meditate on Scripture, the goal isn't to move through as much of the text as possible. Normally, we read at a conversational speed or even faster. That kind of reading is not helpful for meditation.

Suppose I told you that a 24-karat bar of gold was stashed by the side of the road. Imagine that I then gave you the keys to my car and told you that when you found the gold, you could have it. How fast would you drive?

If you were to drive at 70 mph, you would probably miss the bar of gold. Instead, you would need to drive slowly and pay special attention. That's how meditation on God's Word works.

If you want to discover the "gold" in Scripture, *take your time*. If you are accustomed to reading through the Bible in a year, you will have to learn to read slowly. The goal isn't to read the Bible but to let the Bible read you. That doesn't normally happen when we rush through the pages.

Madame Guyon described it this way:

> If you read quickly, it will benefit you little. You will be like a bee that merely skims the surface of a flower. Instead, in this new way of reading with prayer, you must become as the bee who penetrates into the depths of the flower. You plunge deeply within to remove its deepest nectar.[6]

4. Read slowly and with a prayerful heart until a particular word or thought grabs your attention.

Have you ever been reading the Bible when suddenly a verse seemed to jump right off the page and you *knew* that God was talking to you? That happens all the time when we meditate on the Bible. The Divine Lover isn't impressed with how much we can read. He wants to talk to us individually, to express His love to us, to fill us with the awareness of our oneness with Him.

This type of slow, prayerful reading of the Bible is actually an ancient practice known as *lectio divina*. The Latin phrase means "divine reading." It refers to the practice of reading the Bible slowly and with an open heart. This type of reading takes the Bible out of the classroom, where we simply learn, and moves it to the secret places of our lives, where the Divine Lover intimately shares His life and love with us.

When I first began to learn this approach to Scripture, I had been facing some difficult times. Stressful events had been closing in on me in practically every area of my life. One morning I awoke early after a restless night with little sound sleep. I went upstairs into my home office and sat down to read my Bible.

Lord Jesus, I said, *I really could use an encouraging word from You right now. I'm tired. Everything seems to be working against me. Father, speak to me and touch me, will You?*

I opened my Bible and began to read from Psalm 118. I slowly read the first three, four, five verses… then I came to verse six. The first five words of that verse jumped out, grabbing my attention almost as if they were printed in boldface.

"The LORD is for me…" As I reached these words, I heard the voice of my Divine Lover speaking to me. Immediately, I stopped reading further. I took those words and turned them over and over in my mind, emphasizing a different word each time. The *LORD* is for me—I thought about that for a while. I noted that the word LORD was in small caps, indicating that in the original text used the name of God. YHWH, the God who created the heavens and earth, is for me!

Then I emphasized the next word in the statement: "The LORD *is* for me." As I waited in the presence of the Divine Lover, He tenderly assured me that despite all the external evidence to the contrary at that moment, He really *is* for me. Then, "The LORD is *for* me." Again, He lovingly showed me some of what that means. I thought about the apostle Paul's enthusiastic response when he saw the same thing: "If God is for us, who is against us?" (Romans 8:31).

Finally, He took me to the last word in the statement: "The LORD is for *me*." The Divine Creator of all things was speaking to me personally at that moment, assuring me that, among all the things that fall under His jurisdiction, He is for *me* personally!

I've heard and preached thousands of sermons in my lifetime. Most of them I can't even remember. I can't tell you what I've read in many of the books I've bought, but I'll never forget the morning that the Divine Lover spoke to me and told me that *He is for me*. That is only one of many times I have had such an encounter.

Read your Bible slowly, prayerfully, and with an open heart. The Divine Lover will speak to you as you patiently read and wait. When He does, meditate on His words by turning them over and over in your mind until you have tasted their last drop of nectar.

5. As you read the Bible, use "sanctified imagination."
   Project yourself mentally into the story. You probably get caught up in a movie when you watch it. You feel the sadness of the lover with the broken heart. You share the heroine's fear. You sense the thrill of the hero when he defeats the bad guy. In a sense, you become a part of the movie while you watch it.

   Read your Bible that way. In reality, you can identify with the Bible characters much more readily than you can the imaginary characters in a screenplay. After all, the Bible characters were real people, just like you. The way that God worked in their lives is the way He wants to work in your life. You aren't pretending when you place yourself into these Biblical stories because, in some way, their story *is* your story. As Richard Foster advises:

> Seek to live the experience, remembering the
> encouragement of Ignatius of Loyola to apply
> all our senses to our task. Smell the sea. Hear
> the lap of water along the shore. See the crowd.
> Feel the sun on your head and the hunger in
> your stomach. Taste the salt in the air. Touch
> the hem of his garment.[7]

You may be surprised in heaven to discover how much your own experiences parallel those of believers who lived centuries ago. We all have faced the same kinds of fears, doubts, hopes, disappointments, and temptations. To identify with Bible characters isn't a stretch. The only thing that separates you from them is time.

Alexander Whyte affirmed that "the truly Christian imagination never lets Jesus Christ out of her sight...You open your New Testament...And, by your imagination, [at] that moment you are one of Christ's disciples on the spot, and are at His feet."[8]

Use your imagination and become a part of the story as you read it. In doing so, you may experience a touch from the Divine Lover just as they did.

6. Allow the word you hear from the Divine Lover to become a part of you.

Pick up that part of Scripture and treasure it as you would that bar of gold I mentioned earlier. The word that Jesus speaks to you is your greatest treasure. Years from now, you will remember these times when He spoke to you. Solomon, the wisest man who ever lived, said, "A word fitly spoken is like apples of gold in pictures of silver" (Proverbs 25:11 KJV). That's especially true when the word is spoken to you personally by Jesus.

Memorizing what the Divine Lover says to you is a good way to allow His Word to become a part of you. Memorizing Scripture has been a matter of *self-discipline* for many Christians. Some have done it because they felt they ought to do it. They practically grit their teeth with sheer determination.

Imagine the motivation to memorize the Word of God that will come to you as you hear Him personally speak it to you! Legalism demands that you must memorize the Bible. Grace, on the other hand, causes you to *want* to memorize those precious words that the Divine Lover has spoken to you at times of need.

You won't simply be storing Bible verses. Your memory of Scripture will become a file folder containing all the love letters your Divine Lover has sent to you. Who doesn't like to take out old love letters and read them? That's how you will treasure God's Word after you have heard Him speak it to you in love. Scripture memorization under law and under grace are vastly different!

Once the Divine Lover has spoken to you and you have meditated on His Word, take that Word with you throughout your day. In the midst of your busy schedule, think about what He said to you. Turn it over in your mind again throughout the day. You may find yourself smiling as you think about His intimate words to you from the Bible. As you do, you can be assured of something: He's smiling too.

Meditation is a spiritual discipline because it doesn't happen without intention on your part. It isn't hard, but it isn't effortless either. Most of us who grew up in church were programmed with a sense of responsibility toward the Bible. Maybe you have read and studied because you thought you should. Or maybe you sincerely wanted to, but you approached the Bible more like a textbook on theology than a love letter from Someone who passionately loves you. Maybe you haven't used your Bible much because you simply didn't know how to approach the Bible. Or perhaps you resist meditation because it requires you to slow down your actions. To read slowly, to think slowly (meditation) is counter to our present culture and training. But if you give yourself to this discipline, you'll be transformed—that's what the Word of God does.

Meditation is simple, really. If you desire to experience Christ through His Word in this way, you are hearing the invitation of the Divine Lover. Consider meditation a gift from Him. It is a lens through which you may see His lovely face in a clearer and more personal way than you've ever known.

Dear Father,

I want to enjoy You through Your Word. Teach me how to meditate on the Bible until I see Your face and hear Your voice in Scripture. Transform my perspective of the Bible so that I don't see it as a textbook, instruction manual, rule book, or piece of literature. Help me to see it as a love letter. May I become soaked in Your presence and love as I bathe in Your Word. Amen.

6

Identification: Living in Union

THE INWARD SPIRITUAL DISCIPLINES of contemplative prayer and biblical meditation are two effective lenses that allow us to gaze into the loving face of the Christ who dwells within us. However, another inward discipline can help us experience intimacy with Him in a greater way than most believers have ever known. This final inward discipline has many names: "identification with Christ," "union with Christ," and "abiding in Christ." Whatever its name this is the spiritual discipline that has most radically transformed my own life.

Without the revelation and appropriation of this truth in my life, everything I've done to improve myself has proved nothing more than a futile attempt to accomplish the impossible. That is also the testimony of many other Christians down through the ages—men and women such as Andrew Murray, Watchman Nee, Hannah Whitall Smith, and Madame Guyon.

These and countless other believers throughout church history who have understood their union with Christ have reveled in the glorious victory it has brought to their lives.

They found this vital truth to be the cornerstone of victorious Christian living. In fact, Hannah Whitall Smith's classic book on this truth is called *The Christian's Secret of a
Happy Life* and has sold millions of copies since it was
first published in the late nineteenth century. Watchman
Nee referred to this dynamic experience as "the normal
Christian life" in his book by that title. Sadly for most believers, experiencing this union is anything but normal.

If the other spiritual disciplines are lenses through which
we see God's face, understanding the oneness we have
with Christ can be likened to the actual ability to *see* when
we look through those lenses. Our union with Christ helps
us to experience the other rhythms of grace without a
struggle.

The Importance of Union

A believer who hasn't grasped his full identification
with Christ will usually struggle with self-acceptance, sin,
legalism, and ultimately, God. Legalism—doing enough to
be fully approved in God's eyes—always undermines true
spiritual growth. Grace, on the other hand, enables us to
abide in Jesus Christ and simply receive His blessings, not
as a result of *our* works but because of *His* finished work.

Those who don't understand their union with Christ
may appear successful on the surface—much like the religious legalists of Jesus' day who missed His message of
grace. They may know all the right doctrines and attend
or even lead church functions, but inwardly they are essentially lifeless. However, this struggle finally brings some
to the end of themselves when they realize their good
works will never please God.

God never called us to live the Christian life by our
own ability. That's why Christ came into us when we
trusted Him—so that *He* could live through us the life that
we could never live alone. *That's* divine union—the
believer abandoning forever his own attempts to live a

godly life and instead trusting Christ and experiencing the power of His life.

Believers who don't understand divine union may spend years trying to live a victorious life without entering into this divine rest, which is their birthright. Let's consider two main indicators that a Christian isn't conscious of his union with Christ.

Imitating the Life of Christ

In recent years, Christians have renewed their interest in imitating Jesus' example. On the surface, the idea sounds good. However, a study of the New Testament shows that God's goal isn't for us to live *like Christ* but rather *in Christ*. In fact, the New Testament's entire message to believers could be reduced to the two words *in Christ*.

What do we mean when we say that we are in Christ?

We don't mean that we are attempting to copy His lifestyle. To the contrary, we are referring to our union with Him and the expression of His life through us. The Holy Spirit placed you into Christ at salvation so that He could express His life through you. This union was accomplished the moment you believed. It, like everything else in the Christian life, is an undeserved gift.

C.S. Lewis affirms.

> When Christians say the Christ-life is in them, they do not mean simply something mental or moral. When they speak of being "in Christ" or of Christ being "in them," this is not simply a way of saying that they are thinking about Christ or copying Him. They mean that Christ is actually operating through them.[1]

Some will point out that the apostle Paul encouraged the Christians at Corinth to imitate him just as he did Christ (1 Corinthians 11:1). However, the context of all his writings about the believer's union with Jesus Christ clearly shows that Paul didn't believe that anybody should look to Jesus merely as an example to be copied. "The one who joins himself to the Lord is one spirit with Him," Paul wrote (1 Corinthians 6:17).

Paul didn't view Jesus as a historical example to be imitated but as a present reality to be experienced. His strongest confession of his union with Christ is found in Galatians 2:20, where he wrote, "I have been crucified with Christ, and it is no longer I who live, but Christ lives in me; and the life which I now live in the flesh I live by the faith of the Son of God, who loved me and gave Himself up for me."

Think for a moment about this verse. Use the meditation skills from the previous chapter to slowly grasp the full intent of the words, "It is no longer I who live, but Christ lives in me." Paul could not have been any clearer. Biblical faith isn't an attempt to imitate the historical Jesus. It's Jesus living His life through us right now. Identification, not imitation, gives the Christian faith its authenticity. Major Ian Thomas wrote, "The Christian life is the life of the Lord Jesus Christ lived nineteen hundred years ago, *lived now by Him in you!*"[2]

The concept of union with Christ excludes any notion of imitation. Believers who are in union with Jesus Christ participate in His life. As we continuously trust Him, His life is more than an example for our behavior. When we depend on Him, our lifestyle becomes a literal expression of His indwelling presence.

External Rules of Behavior

We don't find the pathway to godly behavior by following outward rules. Because you are a Christian, Jesus Christ literally lives inside you, dwelling in your spirit. Christ is your very life (see Acts 17:28; Colossians 3:4; Philippians 1:21). If Jesus is the source of your life, and if He lives inside you, why would you need to depend on outward voices to tell you how to behave?

Christians naturally want to live in a way that glorifies God. When a person doesn't understand his union with Jesus Christ, he will always be looking for an authority to tell him how to live. His failure to trust the sufficiency of the Christ who dwells inside him will drive him to outside sources for guidance.

Many Christians today look to their church as that source. Some believers evidently don't need the Holy Spirit to guide them—they have their church. Some churches and pastors attempt to micromanage people's lives. I know of churches that dictate everything in their member's lives from how they dress to where they live and work. This type of authoritarian leadership suffocates spiritual growth in people and causes them to remain as spiritual babies, never able to learn to discern the voice of Christ for themselves.

Christians have even abused the Bible and tried to twist it into an external rule book. God's Word does give us guidance in how to live, but the sacred words of Scripture are intended to connect us to Jesus as our life's source. Every book of the Bible is a signpost pointing to Him. The Bible teaches us, but it teaches us to allow Christ to live through us.

The Pharisees made the mistake of living a "Bible-based lifestyle" apart from dependence on God. Their behavior was moral, but they were spiritually dead (John 5:39). A Pharisee who lived 2000 years ago is no different from a sincere Christian in the twenty-first century. When a person reads the Bible solely for the purpose of learning instructions for life, he knows nothing about a living union with Jesus Christ.

Are we to obey the teaching of Scripture?

Of course.

To suggest that believers are to live in union with Christ doesn't diminish the value of biblical instruction at all. Our union with Jesus Christ is the only way to be genuinely obedient. Our own fleshly attempts at obedience are nothing more than dead, religious conformity. To gaze into the face of the Divine Lover requires that we stop struggling to keep rules and simply rest in our relationship.

Man Deified

Our union with Christ does not take away our own human identities. In fact, the life of Jesus Christ within us helps our unique God-given individuality to shine.

"Are you suggesting that I somehow *become* Jesus Christ?" a pastor once asked me.

"Of course not," I responded. "The teaching of our union with Him doesn't nullify our human identity. We don't become deified when Christ takes up residence within us. We still have our mind, will, and emotions. Jesus uses them to express Himself through us to the world."

When sugar is added to a black cup of coffee, the sugar and the coffee become one. The coffee still has its own unique characteristics. It's still coffee, but its nature is changed by its union with the sugar. One might say that the sugar gives new life to the coffee. When a person takes a sip of sweetened coffee, is he drinking coffee or sugar? The answer is both.

When Jesus Christ comes into us at salvation, we don't cease to be human. We do, however, become more than ordinary human beings. We become saints, eternally connected with Jesus Christ. We have a new life and a new divine destiny. Christ's life surges within us. Just as coffee becomes a host to the sugar, we carry the sweet flavor of Jesus to all those we encounter.

Identification Gives Us Our Identity

The Bible talks a lot about our identity. It divides people into two categories (or two identities): those who are "in Adam" and those who are "in Christ." The world has formulated many other artificial distinctions between people, but according to God, our identity is determined by the answer to one single question: To whose family do you belong? The answer to that question is the most important issue of a person's life.

Every human being came into this world as a member of the family of Adam. Being members of his family, we inherited specific family traits. These traits were in our spiritual gene pool. Consider for a moment the universal characteristics of Adam's family.

A Family of Sinners

People don't become sinners the first time they commit a sin any more than a dog becomes a dog the first time it barks. Actions don't determine identity, birth does. All human beings inherit a sin nature from Adam. The Bible teaches that because of his disobedience in the garden of Eden, we all became sinners (Romans 5:19). The common notion that people are basically good directly contradicts the Bible's teaching. (It also contradicts the evening news reports.)

In *The Message*, Eugene Peterson presents Romans 3:10-18 in the following way:

> Basically, all of us, whether insiders or outsiders, start out in identical conditions, which is to say that *we all start out as sinners* [emphasis added]. Scripture leaves no doubt about it:
>
> "There's nobody living right, not even one,
>   nobody who knows the score, nobody alert for God.
> They've all taken the wrong turn;
>   they've all wandered down blind alleys.
> No one's living right;
>   I can't find a single one.
> Their throats are gaping graves,
>   their tongues slick as mud slides.
> Every word they speak is tinged with poison.

>They open their mouths and pollute the air.
>They race for the honor of sinner-of-the-year,
>   litter the land with heartbreak and ruin,
>Don't know the first thing about living with others.
>They never give God the time of day."

Make no mistake about it—you came into this world as a purebred sinner. Just as you received your racial identity from your family tree, you received your spiritual identity from your father, Adam. To believe otherwise is to flatter yourself and to believe a lie (see Romans 3:23, Psalm 58:3).

Spiritually Dead

God created man as a triune being consisting of body, soul, and spirit (1 Thessalonians 5:23). Upon his creation, man was fully alive. His spirit lived inside a healthy body and possessed a soul (mind, will, and emotions), fully animated by divine life.[3]

However, when Adam sinned, he brought the whole human race down with him (Genesis 3; Romans 5:12). At that moment, God's warning that man would die on the very day that he ate from the tree of the knowledge of good and evil became reality.

Adam's body and soul didn't die that day, but his spirit did. His human spirit, which had found its source of life in God alone, suddenly died to God and became filled with sin. He was still a spirit by nature, but his spirit was now animated by sin. Adam's spirit wasn't annihilated; it didn't become nonexistent. Death is separation. In the moment that he sinned, Adam became spiritually separated from God—spiritually dead.

Because Adam contained the "spiritual DNA" for the whole human race, his sin affected us all. When he died spiritually, we all died with him. If your grandfather had physically died when he was a child, you would have died in him. The same is true of our grandfather, Adam. When he died, you died.

Consequently, every person arrives into the world physically alive, but spiritually stillborn. We aren't just spiritually sick when we get here. Our condition is much worse than that. We are born *dead* (see Ephesians 2:1).

Because we were all born in the family line of Adam, we are all sinners. We inherited his sin nature and act accordingly. Even when we are on our best behavior, our actions are sinful in God's sight. Isaiah said, "We're all sin-infected, sin-contaminated. Our best efforts are grease-stained rags" (Isaiah 64:6, THE MESSAGE).

We can do nothing to change the identity we were born with. A person can't be unborn. However, God has a wonderful way of thinking outside the box. We can't be *unborn,* but God devised a way for us to be *reborn.* He made a way for us to die so that we would no longer belong to Adam's family. By His plan, a person can die and then be born again into a different family—a family with a new identity.

Our New Identification with Christ

Your heavenly Father has such a passionate desire for eternal companionship with you that He developed a God-sized plan to ensure that you became His. This amazing plan demonstrates that He considered no price too great to have a loving relationship with you. Consider the thrilling proactive steps the Divine Lover has taken to guarantee that you would forever belong to Him.

God Chose You

Before you were born, when you hadn't even had one chance to prove yourself worthy of God's love by doing a single good deed, God decided that He wanted you for Himself (Romans 9:8-11). In the quietness of eternity past, before time even existed, He saw you and determined to pour out His love for you forever (Ephesians 1:4).

Have you thought about why you are a Christian today? Did some intrinsic virtue in you cause you to believe in Christ while others don't? Not at all. God decided a long time ago that *He wanted you.* He alone is the reason you know Him today. Nobody naturally seeks after God (Romans 3:11). Before you ever gave God a thought, He had been thinking of you. He *chose* you.

Jesus was clear about this. He told His disciples, "You did not choose Me but I chose you" (John 15:16). The only reason we love Him at all is "because He first loved us" (1 John 4:19). The first step toward your identification with Christ is knowing that you have been divinely chosen.

God knew you would never come to Him on your own. So He did the unimaginable: He came to you! The Creator of the universe laid aside His robes of royalty and clothed Himself in a human body so that He could invade the earth and rescue you from the world, the flesh, and the devil (see Philippians 2:5-8). A perfect God stepped into an imperfect world to pursue you. Personified Purity waded into magnified perversion because of His great love for you.

The angels of heaven may have asked in disbelief, "You're going to do *what?*" They would not be able to comprehend how a holy God could love you so much that He would leave heaven and come to earth just to pursue you. But God had made up His mind that you would be His, and God always accomplishes His will (Daniel 4:35).

God Drew You to Himself

Do you remember when you first began to consider the claims of Christ? Up until that time, you didn't seek to know Him. Maybe you had no interest whatsoever in spiritual things. Maybe you held a sense of religious respect toward Him, but being a Christian wasn't high on your list of goals.

Then things changed. Do you remember when you found your thoughts moving toward Jesus? You found yourself thinking in completely new ways. Your interest in Christ began to grow until you were actually *attracted* to Him.

What brought about the change? Had some spiritual virtue within you been lying dormant? Not according to the Bible. Remember the passage already quoted from Romans 3. Until the Holy Spirit begins to draw us to Christ, we never give God the time of day. Jesus Himself said, "No one can come to Me unless the Father who sent Me draws him" (John 6:44).

You are a Christian because the Divine Lover drew you by His love. He miraculously stirred you to life and caused you to want Him. You would never have wanted Him on your own. His love alone initiates and consummates our salvation.

Jesus loves you enough to supernaturally draw you to Himself. By revealing His beauty and His passion for you, He loved you until you loved Him right back! You are a Christian for one simple reason—Jesus Christ decided that He wanted you and wouldn't give up until you were His.

What about *your* will in salvation? Don't we exercise our own free will? The following marriage metaphor might help answer that question.

Suppose a husband has a desire for physical intimacy with his wife one morning, but she's not in the mood. However, he knows her well and knows how to "put her in the mood." So he determines to change her mind through the course of the day.

He has heard Gary Smalley say that "lovemaking begins in the kitchen," so he washes dishes after mealtime, telling her to relax, assuring her that he'll handle it all. He has heard James Dobson teach that women want to feel valued, so he expresses sincere verbal appreciation for his wife. He remembers reading Tim LaHaye's suggestion that women want romance, not just sex. So he leaves a red rose and a love note on his wife's pillow before she goes to the bedroom that night.

All throughout the day and the evening, this husband diligently expresses love to his wife in nonphysical ways. He takes these steps because he sincerely loves her. However, he does want a particular response from her. He acts toward her in ways that he knows she will understand as expressions of love from him.

That night, he holds her in his arms. He begins to tenderly kiss her...Maybe I should stop there. Do you know what happens then? Her will is changed. Because of her husband's love for her and the effective ways he has expressed it all day, she finds that her will has been changed to align with His will. She is *ravished* (see Proverbs 5:18-19 KJV) by her husband's love.

We may ask. Whose will determined how the events of the night unfolded—his or hers?

She definitely exercised her choice in the matter. However, her will had been taken captive by her husband's love until it became one with his will. You might say that his enticing love refused to be satisfied until her will was "brought to life" to align with His.

Jesus loves you so much that He orchestrated the details of your life to guarantee that your will, which was "dead" to Him, would come alive. He gave you a will to know Him. Otherwise, you never would have wanted Him at all. The Bible says, "But as many as received Him, to them He gave the right to become children of God, even those who believe in His name, who were born, not of blood, nor of the will of the flesh *nor of the will of man,* but of God" (John 1:12-13, emphasis added).

God Gave You a New Identity

When you received Jesus Christ, your family history changed. God took you out of the family of Adam and placed you into His own family. How did this transaction take place? It happened through the power of the cross.

Perhaps you have believed that only three people were crucified at Calvary—Jesus and the two thieves. The Bible teaches that they weren't the only ones crucified that day. You were crucified too. The person you were while in the family of Adam was crucified with Jesus Christ and is no longer alive.

The New Testament teaches repeatedly that the old identity we had in Adam has been forever removed from us by the cross. Paul often wrote on the matter, saying that he had been crucified and no longer lived (Galatians 2:20), that our old self (the person we were in Adam) was crucified with Jesus (Romans 6:6), and that we have died and our life is now "hidden with Christ in God" (Colossians 3:3). Scripture tells us many times that the person we were before we knew Christ is now dead (see Romans 6:2,4,7-8,11,13; 7:2-4,6,8; Colossians 2:20).

You not only died with Jesus Christ but also participated with Him in His burial and resurrection (see Romans 6:4; Colossians 2:12). The life you had in Adam is now dead and buried. When Jesus Christ rose from the dead, you rose with Him to walk in a new life—His life! The old you no longer lives. Now Christ lives in you. The life you now live is by faith in Him.

Your *identification* with Jesus Christ's death and resurrection is the single cause for the union you now share with Him. The Godward gaze is possible by looking inward to the indwelling Christ and trusting Him to animate your life. He is now your very life. Religious systems reach up toward God through self-effort. But to experience God's grace is to realize that He has reached down to you and has joined Himself together with you in a union that will never be broken.

Union and Spiritual Disciplines

To maintain a Godward gaze, we must rest in the union we have with Jesus Christ. The importance of this can't be overstated. Only a confident realization that Christ is the very essence of our lives will enable the Christian to fully enjoy the intimacy our Divine Lover longs to share. We live in union with Christ as we continuously appropriate the truth of our new identity in Him. This is a spiritual discipline that God longs for us all to experience as He teaches us about our identification with Christ in His death and resurrection.

John Calvin observed:

> It is a mystery of Christ's secret union with the devout which is by nature incomprehensible. If anybody should ask me how this communion takes place, I am not ashamed to confess that it is a secret too lofty for either my mind to comprehend or my words to declare. And to speak more plainly, I would rather experience than understand it.[4]

This is an interesting perspective from one of church history's most noted theologians. Calvin's attitude is a good example for believers today. In this lifetime, we will never fully understand the union we share with Christ, but don't let that keep you from experiencing the benefits of it!

Understanding who we are in Christ as a result of our co-crucifixion and co-resurrection with Him transformed my life in 1990. This is the foundation for every other spiritual discipline by which I enjoy intimacy with Jesus Christ today. To the extent that I have lived out my union with Him, I have seen the loving face of God with greater clarity than I had ever known.

In the introduction, I defined spiritual disciplines as biblical practices, motived by love and practiced in faith, that help us experience a deeper sense of intimacy with

God than we could otherwise know. The biblical practice of *identification* happens when we appropriate, by faith, the truth that God has taken us out of Adam's family and given us a new identity in Jesus Christ.

You can become a partaker of the divine nature of Christ (see 2 Peter 1:3-4). His life is now yours. *You don't have to struggle to live a Christian life anymore.*

Just relax and watch Jesus live His life in and through you every day.

LOOKING UPWARD

1. Read Romans 6. Ask the Holy Spirit to reveal the meaning of your identification with Christ in His crucifixion and resurrection.

   Martin Luther wrote about the book of Romans,

   > This letter is truly the most important piece in the New Testament. It is purest Gospel. It is well worth a Christian's while not only to memorize it word for word but also to occupy himself with it daily, as though it were the daily bread of the soul. It is impossible to read or to meditate on this letter too much or too well.[5]

   As you read from this important chapter in Romans, pray to receive revelation about these truths. Record your impressions in your notebook.

   a. You died to sin (6:2).

   b. You have been raised to walk in newness of life (6:4).

   c. Your old self was crucified with Him (6:6).

    d. Sin won't dominate you any more because
      you are under grace now, not law (6:14).

    e. You have been freed from sin and are now
      a slave of righteousness (6:17-18).

    Look at each response that you have given. Do your answers suggest that God alone gets all the glory for what has happened in your life, or do they indicate that you deserve some of the credit? In what ways do your responses reflect a different understanding than you had before you studied Romans 6?

2. Write a declaration of your identification with Jesus Christ in His death and resurrection.

    The following is an example of what you might write: "I affirm by faith that the person I was in Adam no longer exists. The old me was crucified with Jesus Christ. I was buried with Him and have been raised to a new life. I have no life of my own anymore. He is my Life. By God's enabling grace, I will continuously trust Jesus Christ to express His life in me and through me from this day forward."

3. Pray and ask Jesus Christ to speak to you and tell you what He thinks about you.

    Jesus chose you to be His so that He could pour out His love on you for all eternity. Have you ever *personally* heard Him express His thoughts about you? If you pray and hear nothing, don't be fooled into thinking He isn't speaking. Learning to recognize His voice may take some time and practice. Pray, asking the same thing every day, until you do hear Jesus tell you in specific and personal terms how He feels about you.

Does this seem self-centered? It isn't. In your own relationships with those you deeply love, don't you find fulfillment in sharing your love with them and seeing them embrace that love? In the most meaningful relationships, two people give *and* receive meaningful expressions of love. To deeply enjoy the union you have with Christ, develop the practice of giving *and* receiving love.

In your notebook, write a short paragraph describing Jesus' attitude toward you as a result of your union with Him.

Dear Father,

I am thrilled that You have chosen me. Thank You for placing me on the cross too, and for giving me an identity that is grounded in Your life and not my former self. Teach me to rest in You and trust You as my life source. May Your life flow through me as a natural rhythm of grace that carries me through my day, every day of my life. Amen.

Part Three
The Outward Look

7

Creativity:
An Unassuming Voice

I WAS STANDING ON THE CANADIAN SIDE of Niagara Falls, looking over a short wall, watching the water fall 170 feet to the river below. Melanie and I had driven to this famous site after speaking at a conference in nearby Toronto. As we stood together, watching the awesome rush of the water, we had to lean over and speak right into each other's ear in order to be heard above the roar of the falls. The sheer force of the water pouring over the edge was amazing.

We looked below and saw a ferry at the base of the falls. *The Maid of the Mist* is available to take tourists into the area surrounded by the horseshoe-shaped falls. As soon as we saw the boat, we knew that we wanted to see Niagara Falls from that angle. To see it from the safety of the platform above was one thing, but to see it from below would be a different matter altogether.

Soon we found ourselves aboard *The Maid of the Mist*, wearing raincoats and huddling together with other tourists who wanted to get a closer look. The boat began to slowly make its way toward the center of the falls. As we drew closer, I began to experience a sense of awe I had never known.

The misty spray caused by the falling water slamming into the river settled on our faces. I had only *thought* the falls were loud from above. Now, at the edge of the place where the water all came crashing down and created a swirling whirlpool, it seemed almost deafening.

As we stood without speaking, I experienced feelings I had never felt before. On one hand, I liked being this close to the falls. The beauty was compelling. The force of the water was awesome. The falls were irresistible. I wanted us to move in closer, but on the other hand, I began to sense what can only be described as fear.

Looking upward toward the top of the falls where we had stood earlier, I was amazed at how much farther the distance seemed looking up than it did looking down. Niagara's height was amazing. Its strength was awesome. Its beauty, unequaled. Standing before the falls, all I could say was, "Wow! This is awesome!" And even that seemed inadequate.

Later, as I reminisced about our experience aboard *The Maid of the Mist,* I remembered that Niagara Falls is just one of the many ways that the Divine Lover reveals Himself to those who have eyes to see. Once again, God was speaking through nature in an unassuming way to those who have ears to hear.

My reaction at the bottom of Niagara Falls is similar to the reaction of people who draw near to God. Sometimes our awe is so great that it resembles fear. We are irresistibly attracted to Him, yet we are deeply aware of our own smallness next to His imposing power and beauty. Our God *is* an awesome God. We find ourselves wanting to run to Him and hide from Him at the same time.

At Niagara Falls, God dramatically spoke through nature to me about His great power and creativity. Through the years, God has spoken powerfully through a sunset (remember that beautiful sunset in Mexico God used to remind me of His faithfulness?), a gently flowing brook, or His celestial handiwork in the stars above. Christians are likely to be able to recount some memorable experiences when God spoke to them powerfully through His creation. I'm sure if I asked you, you'd tell me about that time when...well, you get the idea.

God Creates Something Out of Nothing

In the first two parts of this book, we learned to gaze into the Divine Lover's face by looking upward and inward. In this last section, I want to challenge you to experience intimacy with Him by looking *outward*.

Perhaps we can most clearly see and appreciate the Divine Lover's face through the universe He created for us. The spiritual discipline here is practicing the habit of seeing Him through *creativity*—all of which ultimately finds its source in God.

The word *creativity* finds its root in the word *create*, which means "to bring into existence something out of nothing." The ability to create always finds its ultimate source in God, for He alone is the Creator of all things. Created things (such as human beings) can't create unless they are *endowed* with creative ability. Like everything else vested in man from the beginning, our ability to create has been contaminated by sin, but it is still a gift from God. We cannot boast about the creative talents God has given us. Our creative abilities are imperfect reflections of His *perfect* creativity.

Those who enjoy a continuous Godward gaze recognize His unassuming voice speaking through creativity. God has often spoken to people through His creation. He can make Himself known through thunder (1 Samuel 7:10), lightning (Exodus 19:16), fire (Exodus 13:21), a bush (Exodus 3:2), the skies and land (Psalm 19:1), and even a talking donkey (Numbers 22:28). The list could go on and on.

Everything in nature testifies to the presence of God in this world. Romans 1:20 teaches that although God is invisible, we can clearly see His existence in creation. In the end, nobody will have an excuse for their unbelief because nature itself proves His reality. We truly live in a God-bathed world.

And God reveals Himself not only in nature but also in our own human creativity. Sometimes He shows up in the most unexpected places, secretly smiling at those who have eyes to see Him through the elements of our culture.

Did you know that the Divine Lover is often standing right in the middle of the ordinary cultural elements we see every day? I believe He takes great joy in suddenly revealing Himself to us in unexpected places at unexpected times as He did to the disciples who walked with Him on the Emmaus Road (Luke 24).

Surprise! It's Me!

Shortly after I was married, my parents and younger sister moved out of the country for five years because of my dad's work responsibilities. I only saw them once during that five-year period. I was 19 when they left, and I deeply missed them. I looked forward to seeing them more than words could express.

When the time drew near for their return to the States, my dad arrived a few days ahead of my mom and sister without telling me he was coming early. I had been out to lunch, and as I pulled into the parking lot of the church where I was serving as pastor, I saw my dad sitting in his car. But because I wasn't expecting to see him, I didn't recognize him. In fact, I didn't really pay any attention to him. I casually glanced at him and parked my car.

When I began to walk toward the building, my dad spoke. "Hey there, young man," he said. Instantly, I recognized his voice. I whirled around and ran toward him. It was one of the great thrills in my life, and I'm sure my dad enjoyed suddenly surprising me with his presence.

That's how Jesus Christ acts toward you. Sometimes He wears the icons of our culture like a disguise. He hides Himself from the world—from those who don't want to see Him—but at unexpected moments He suddenly pulls down the mask and gives those He loves a clear glimpse of His face. At those moments, those who love Him squeal with excitement, "Jesus, it's *You!* I see *You* in that!" I have no doubt that when this happens, He laughs with delight.

Will you ask the Holy Spirit to help you gaze into the Divine Lover's face in the ordinary, everyday icons of life? You will be thrilled when He enables you to look beyond the superficial and see the supernatural. Jesus is waiting to surprise you with His presence. Open your eyes to see Him in the everyday icons of culture.

What are these cultural icons? They are common expressions of human creativity. Let's consider some of the "secular" images in our society that can become sacred ground when we recognize Jesus in the midst of them.

Hearing Him in Music

Perhaps no medium on earth has the capacity to affect a person's emotions like music. People have used music throughout history to move others into action. It has motivated men to charge forward into battle. It has prepared couples to make love. Music has caused some to sit in reflection and caused others to get up and dance. It has soothed fussy babies until they drifted off into a peaceful sleep. It has been used at weddings to celebrate a new life together and years later at funerals to grieve the end of that shared life. Music has been a comforting companion to prisoners and slaves. It has given expression to a celebration of victory. Certain music has even increased the amount of milk a cow gives! Music can make us laugh or cry. It can give us feelings of nostalgia, joy, hope, sadness, and even anger. Its power is incredible.

Music was born in heaven, flowing from the very heart of God. It framed the universe at the beginning of time. When God laid the foundation of the earth, "the morning stars sang together and all the sons of God shouted for joy" (Job 38:7).

A simple word search in the Bible shows that God likes *singing*. In both the Old and New Testaments, we are encouraged to sing to the Lord. The Psalmist said, "Come before Him with joyful singing" (Psalm 100:2). The apostle Paul said that believers are to be "singing and making melody with your heart to the Lord" (Ephesians 5:19).

Singing has a prominent place in the Bible among God's family of faith. It has also been the hallmark of many great moments in our lives. Consider the role that singing played in just a few of the pivotal moments in the history of God's people.

- When God delivered Moses and the children of Israel from Egypt, they walked through the Red Sea on dry land. When they reached the other side, they sang together. In fact, Exodus 15 is called "The Song of Moses" to this day.

- The people of Israel sang as they dedicated the city wall around Jerusalem that had been rebuilt under the leadership of Nehemiah (Nehemiah 12:40-42).

- When the ark of the covenant was returned to Israel, singers were appointed to mark the occasion. As they sang, King David danced with delight (1 Chronicles 15:26-29).

- Paul and Silas sang in a Philippian jail at midnight, and God caused an earthquake to shake open the prison doors (Acts 16:25-26).

Singing is a way to express the consuming passion of our hearts. The melody and tempo of a song enhance the content of the message. A girl appreciates a young man who tells her he loves her, but if he *sings* to her, she can be absolutely giddy.

Singing preceded this world and will outlast it. Music will be an integral part of our lives in heaven (Revelation 5:9; 14:3; 15:3). God obviously has a real affinity for music.

So we are not surprised that we can gaze into the face of the Divine Lover through the lens of music. Certain songs move me deeply and lead to an awesome sense of intimacy with my Father. I seldom hear or sing "The Love of God," "Great Is Thy Faithfulness," or "A Mighty Fortress Is Our God" without choking up. The great hymns of the faith often teach us theology as well as touch us in the deep places of our heart.

Many modern praise choruses also facilitate a deeper sense of intimacy with the Divine Lover. Unfortunately, some modern choruses contain a weak or aberrant theology, but many can be useful for praising God and experiencing Him in a fresh way. A good chorus lifts your heart toward heaven.

Jesus Outside the Church Doors

Don't make the mistake of thinking that you can only hear the Divine Lover's voice in religious music. Remember, He can make Himself known to you in unlimited ways. He isn't about to surrender everything outside the church doors to the world. Music written apart from His life is pirated material, and the Divine Lover can reclaim it anytime He wants.

I was speaking on this subject at a conference one day when I asked the group, "Are you able to hear God speak to you if there is no religious tone to what you hear?" The audience waited for me to continue. "Close your eyes and listen to the song I'm about to play," I encouraged them.

"Perhaps you have heard the song before, but this time, listen for the voice of the Divine Lover in it."

Then, at a spiritual retreat, in a room filled with Christians, I played a recording by a well-known rock singer, Joe Cocker. The song is called "You Are So Beautiful to Me." The lyrics tenderly express the great love and admiration of the singer for his love.

As the song played, grown men and women began to cry. For the first time, many were hearing their Divine Lover's voice from a source they had never thought to consider before now. For every person there, this song would never again be the same. God's love had redeemed it and brought it into the kingdom as a gift for those who listened.

Does this concept make you uncomfortable? If so, consider this question: Why should Jesus Christ be restricted to communicating to you only in religious ways? He is Lord over all the earth and can use anything He chooses to express love to those who are His. One unmarried lady I know says that she listens to a radio station that plays nothing but romantic love songs and that she often hears the Lord sing to her through those songs. Who would tell her she is wrong?

I have experienced supernatural joy at times when I have heard certain nonreligious music. I was enthralled as I watched a live performance of the musical *The Phantom of the Opera*. On another occasion, tears filled my eyes as I attended a concert by the great Italian singer, Andrea Bocelli, despite the fact that not one word was sung in English.

Don't misunderstand me. I'm not suggesting that every time we have a positive feeling, God is manifesting Himself to us. I recognize that our emotions can be manipulated by various influences. However, I also believe that Christians are sometimes guilty of dismissing the pervasive presence of Christ in this world by labeling experiences that aren't directly religious as "nonspiritual."

I can almost imagine that when I listened to Andrea Bocelli in concert, Jesus was saying, *Isn't this great? Steve, I love seeing how you enjoy this concert. I can't wait until you come home to be here with Me. I have even better ones waiting for you here!*

My friend Cheryl said that as she listened to an unbeliever sing a song, she asked the Lord, *Why have you given such great talent to people who don't even know you?* She said that the Lord simply answered, *To bring you pleasure.*

The Lord showed another friend, Terry, our foolishness in living like we are spiritually impoverished when, in reality, we are rich in Jesus Christ. The Lord used the theme song from *The Beverly Hillbillies* television show. Do you remember the theme song about Jed's luck in striking oil one day when he was hunting for some food? Instantly he became a rich man.

Terry heard Jesus in this song, singing about our feeble attempts to live the Christian life out of the self-imposed poverty of our own strength. He heard the Divine Lover say, "You're a millionaire!" Then, regarding walking after the flesh—"Move away from there!"

When I heard his illustration, I was amused and wrote my own verse that described how I felt when I first realized the riches I have in Christ. The revelation came, and...

> The first thing I knew I said, "I'm a millionaire!"
> I looked at my flesh and thought, "I'm not living there!
> Abiding in Jesus is where I want to be!
> I'll renounce the flesh, and rest in Him for all eternity...."
> The Grace Walk, that is—His sufficiency—His Life.
> Y'all trust Him now, ya hear?

Do these examples sound silly to you? Remember, the Divine Lover lives with us where we are and speaks the language of our lives. Do you have a concept of God that allows Him to express Himself to you in unexpected ways, even in ways that aren't "religious"?

Jesus at the Movies

In the movie *Contact,* Jodie Foster plays a scientist who is whisked away to another planet in a special spaceship built with blueprints provided by extraterrestrials. In the scene where she makes contact with the aliens, she is carried through one space wormhole after another until she finds herself standing beside a beautiful ocean on a distant planet.

The beach where she stands is an awesome and beautiful place. In her first moments in this otherworldly paradise, she gasps with amazement while tears of joy stream down her cheeks. She has tried to document her journey in technical terms for her fellow researchers who selected her to make the trip. Her journey has been scientific and academic. But now, as she tries to take it all in, her scientific paradigm fails her. She stands riveted in one spot, overwhelmed by the beauty, and simply whispers through tears of joy, "They should have sent a poet."

"They should have sent a poet," said Jodie Foster's character. So it is with the love of God. Theologians can't describe Him. Books can't contain Him. Sermons and songs don't do Him justice. His love is immeasurable, immutable, and irrevocable. Being supernatural, His love can't be understood by natural minds or natural means. It overflows the bounds of human experience and defies adequate explanation. A chimpanzee could sooner teach molecular biology than could a man do justice to explaining the scope of God's love.

Divine love makes no sense to the natural mind. It so drastically transcends the pallid experience that man calls love that it almost seems a violation of the word for humans to use it. His love outpaces human love to the point of absurdity when judged by common man using common sense.

Divine love passionately ravages the senses of God's chosen ones and leaves us absolutely breathlessly in love with Him. Let those of us who have an ear to hear *listen* as He whispers sweet affirmations in a hundred ways every day. Let us open our eyes and *see* the beauty of His presence in every detail of our lives. Let's *taste* and see that the Lord is good in the countless ways He reveals His love to us. May we *feel* the gentle touch of His loving hand in the places where we hurt. And *smell* His sweet fragrance as He holds us in His arms and swears that He will never let us go, even for a moment.

I want to allow the greatness of His love to engulf me. I don't want to resist it. I want the finite experiences of my life to be swallowed up by infinite love. I want to take my eyes off my circumstances and look at Him. I want to stop worrying about tomorrow and look at Him. I want to turn away from regrets about the past and look at Him. Those things that distract me, disturb me, dilute me...I want to turn away from it all and look at Him. As I reflect on his love, only one question comes to mind—where's a good poet when you need one?

I wrote the preceding paragraphs after I watched *Contact* and considered the frustration Jodie Foster's character experienced trying to describe what she had seen. Those of us who gaze upon the face of Jesus must also struggle to describe Him. Theologians, preachers, authors —none of us can capture it. Words aren't enough.

Some Christians believe movies are "from the devil." "Hollywood" is snarled from the lips of some believers as if it left the taste of bile in their mouths. "Can anything good come out of Hollywood?" they ask.

Surely, the movie industry is marketing some abominable productions. But are we to summarily dismiss films as being outside the realm where God can work and speak? Can and will the Divine Lover speak to us through this particular cultural medium? I believe that He will.

I admit that I'm a movie buff. I've always enjoyed movies, except for a few dark years when "I gave up everything for God" but chewing gum (and I had questions about that). Once I finally realized that I didn't have to live a lifestyle of self-flagellation to prove something to God or myself, I began to enjoy movies again.

My wife, Melanie, tells me that I can get a sermon out of any movie. I don't watch movies looking for spiritual applications. I just see them. I have seen the Divine Lover smiling at me between the scenes, whispering secrets between the actors' lines. Maybe others in the theater didn't see Him, but I know what I saw.

In the movie *Chocolat,* I saw the power of authentic grace over religious legalism. In *Les Misérables,* I became teary watching the effect of unconditional love and forgiveness on Jean Valjean. In *The Legend of Bagger Vance,* Will Smith's character reminded me that I already have everything I need in Christ. All I need to do is find my "authentic swing" by trusting in what He has already given me by His life. The list of movies could continue. In many, I unexpectedly heard the voice and saw the face of the Divine Lover. I know Jesus goes to the movies. I've seen Him there.

As you watch contemporary films, remember that the movie might be a parable for you. Jesus used parables (fictional stories) to explain spiritual realities when He taught His disciples. He will do the same thing today as He teaches you more about His life, His grace, and His love. This is seeing God through the creative gift He has given others.

You don't have to *try* to find something "spiritual" in a movie. All the world is God's pulpit. Just relax and enjoy the show. He will reveal Himself to you more and more as you learn to be open to divine whispers in the ordinary places of life.

Seeing His Face in Art

I've never been particularly "artsy." Melanie dragged me to the Museum of Art in Atlanta to see Monet's work. I went with her to the Rijksmuseum when we ministered in Amsterdam. I saw paintings done by the Masters. I understand that they are masterpieces, and I sincerely tried to "get it," but I just couldn't.

I stood staring as if I knew what I was looking at, hoping that the beauty would emerge like one of those three-dimensional pictures that become clear if you look long enough. But nothing happened. "The depth of conflict overpowers you," one observer noted as we stood together staring at a painting. "I can hardly bear it," I answered. But I just didn't get it.

Elvis on velvet or "Dogs Playing Poker"—I recognize a little talent there. But surrealist paintings by Jean Arp? Or expressionism by Max Beckmann? French fauvism by Matisse? I'm sorry. Swahili makes more sense to me.

However, one day I read a book that had a tremendous spiritual impact on me. The book was about a particular piece of art—*The Return of the Prodigal Son* by Rembrandt. Henri Nouwen's book of the same name is a description of the insight the Divine Lover gave to Nouwen as they sat together at the Hermitage Museum in Saint Petersburg while Nouwen visited Russia.

While Nouwen sat for hours looking at the masterpiece by Rembrandt, the Divine Lover started him on a long spiritual adventure. As he watched the changing light and shadows on the painting as the day progressed, the art became the voice of His heavenly Father showing Him that the painting was really about *him.*

The voice of the Divine Lover drew Nouwen's attention first to the younger son. There Nouwen learned about returning home and being a son. Then his attention was directed toward the elder brother, who stood by with clasped hands and a closed heart. Nouwen heard the Beloved's voice speak to him about the levels of rivalry and doubt in his own life. At last, he was drawn toward the father in Rembrandt's painting. There he learned lessons about loving unconditionally and receiving those who have wandered far away from home.

Nouwen concluded his writing about what the Divine Lover said to him through Rembrandt:

> When four years ago, I went to Saint Petersburg to see Rembrandt's *The Return of the Prodigal Son*, I had little idea how much I would have to live what I then saw. I stand with awe at the place where Rembrandt brought me. He led me from the kneeling, disheveled young son to the standing, bentover old father, from the place of being blessed to the place of blessing. As I look at my own aging hands, I know that they have been given to me to stretch out toward all who suffer, to rest upon the shoulders of all who come, and to offer the blessing that emerges from the immensity of God's love.[1]

Throughout history, our loving Father has used artists to enable us to gaze into His own face more clearly. Michelangelo poured himself into his work for the glory of God. Other artists have created works for His glory alone.

In our own day, many artists' works showcase the glory of God. Only eternity will reveal how the Divine Lover has reached out to tenderly touch lives through the paintings of these artistic oracles of His love. In their work is a subtle expression of the lovely face of Jesus.

Perhaps the beauty of art is a sneak preview of the beauty that awaits us in the honeymoon home our Divine Lover is preparing for us at this very moment. In our own day, we have Thomas Kinkade, known as the Painter of Light. He indeed does point us to The Light. I have stared into some of his paintings and wished that I could go there. I've felt as if I'd like to step right into the picture, if possible.

C.S. Lewis describes this experience in *The Weight of Glory*. He wrote:

> We want something else which can hardly be put into words—to be united with the beauty we see, to pass into it, to receive it into ourselves, to bathe in it, to become part of it.... At present we are on the outside of the world, the wrong side of the door. We discern the freshness and purity of morning, but they do not make us fresh and pure. We cannot mingle with the splendors we see. But all the leaves of the New Testament are rustling with the rumor that it will not always be so. Some day, God willing, we shall get in.[2]

Music, movies, and art are three common cultural icons that identify our contemporary culture. Others exist, of course. Great novels sometimes reveal spiritual truth more powerfully than nonfiction. Poetry, dance, sculpture, or even the more common creative endeavors such as sewing, quiltmaking, cooking, woodworking...the list of ways God can express Himself through creativity goes on and on. When you understand that He speaks through creativity, the Holy Spirit will be able to teach you how to hear His unassuming voice within your daily routine, your lifestyle, and the culture around you. Practice the discipline of seeing the face of your Divine Lover in the midst of all that He's created—His handiwork of nature or the artistry of contemporary culture. Through both, He takes delight in surprising us with manifestations of His presence and love.

LOOKING UPWARD

1. In your notebook, write a description of a place where you have experienced the presence of God through nature.

   What "Niagara Falls experience" comes to your mind? This world is a collage of places that reveal the creativity of the Divine Lover. What is your favorite place in nature to experience intimate times with Jesus Christ?

   Seek out a place in nature near your home where you can withdraw and spend time alone with Jesus. When you go to this place alone, take your notebook and open your heart for the Lord to speak to you through the things you see and hear.

2. Identify songs that cause you to experience a sense of intimacy with Jesus Christ.

   What are your favorite hymns? Choruses? Find a place where you can be alone and sing them aloud to the Lord. Pick a song, write down the words, and read them as a prayer to the Lord.

What are your favorite nonreligious songs? Listen to them again and ask the Divine Lover to sing to you through those songs. Do you have favorite nonreligious songs that you can sing to Him? If singing your favorite songs to Jesus or asking Him to sing them to you would be blasphemous, you might want to consider listening to different music (Philippians 4:8). Why listen to music that weakens your faith and distracts your focus from Jesus?

3. Write down your top five favorite movies.

Think about the story line of each film. List the spiritual applications you could make if you were to view the movies as parables. Consider the following questions as you recall each movie:

- Did the movie contain a message about love? If so, what was the message, and how can it relate to your relationship to your Divine Lover?

- What was the conflict in the movie? What does this movie say about the appropriate way to resolve conflict in your own life?

- What characteristics of God could you learn about from this movie? His sovereignty? His love? His patience? His goodness?

As you consider these questions, don't look only at the superficial plot of the movie. Look for deeper meaning. For instance, the movie *Bagger Vance* was about a character named Junuh learning how to get back his golf swing. That was the plot on a superficial level. However, on a spiritual level, the movie could be seen as a parable about winning the game of life by trusting the sufficiency of Christ, which every Christian already possesses.

4. Identify a particular piece of art that you find attractive. It may be a painting, a sculpture, or any other type of visual art.

   Why are you attracted to that particular piece of art? Give the Divine Lover time to speak to you as He did to Henri Nouwen as he studied Rembrandt's painting. Ask the Holy Spirit to speak to you from this work and to show you things about Jesus. Ask Him to show you things about yourself. Write down the things He tells you.

5. Has God given you a special talent? How is God's creative gift expressed in you? If you've been raised with legalism, you may be reluctant to let your creative gifts shine. Write a brief paragraph exploring your own desire to be creative. If you don't recognize any specific creative abilities in yourself, let that admission be your prayer.

The purpose of this chapter and these final exercises is to encourage you to broaden your field of view as you gaze into the lovely face of your Father. Most Christians are familiar with religious ways to see the face of God. You can also experience Him in the ordinary flow of your life through the common icons of contemporary culture.

Ask Him to show you other places where you may gaze into His face. Then go out into each day with your eyes wide open in eager anticipation that the Divine Lover will step out of the shadows of contemporary experiences just so that you can see His smile. He wants you to see Him all throughout your day, whispering in the midst of crowded places and schedules, saying, *I just wanted to tell you again—I love you.*

Dear Father,

Open my eyes so that I will see You in the world around me all through the day. Teach me to recognize Your face and voice in the midst of the ordinary. May I increasingly understand that all the world is a pulpit from which You declare Your love for me. Give me eyes to see and ears to hear. I know that You love me, but I enjoy hearing You tell me again and again. Surprise me with Your love, Lord. I'll be watching and listening. Amen.

8

Service:
Keeping Our Eyes
Wide Open

WHEN BOB AND JILL WERE TALKING ONE DAY shortly after their first wedding anniversary, Bob brought up an idea. "I've been thinking about it," he began. "I need help around here. With the heavy work schedule I have, I can't keep up with all the things that need to be done around the house. Take the yard, for instance—if I had a son, in time, he could mow the lawn. He could keep the weeds out of the flower bed, clean out the garage, wash my car...."

"Funny you should mention that," Jill answered. "I've been having similar thoughts. I could use help with the laundry, cooking, and other responsibilities at home that take up a big part of my time."

"That settles it then," Bob said. "Let's start a family!"

Obviously, this is not the way couples dream about their children. People don't have children so that they will have somebody to help them with the chores. If they did, they would certainly be disappointed in the days ahead!

Although the imaginary conversation described above sounds ridiculous, many of God's children think that way about God and His family. Some believe that the reason God decided to have children is so that we can serve Him. They believe that the primary reason they are Christians is that God needs them to help Him with things He wants to accomplish in this world.

Some churches are built around the motto, "Saved to Serve." These Christians live under the notion that they are the only hands, feet, eyes, and ears that God has in this world. To them, Christian service is a duty that must be discharged if they are to fulfill the purpose of their salvation.

Perhaps no aspect of believers' lives is more vulnerable to legalism than their Christian service. In churches all over the world, preachers load Christians with guilt because of their lack of service. But this overshadowing sense of shame will actually destroy all motivation to serve the Lord.

Two Extremes

We do well to avoid extreme approaches to Christian service, for they will block our view of the smiling face of the Divine Lover. We have already seen one extreme: the idea that God needs us and that we must actively serve in order to meet His minimum requirements for our lives.

The biblical truth on this matter shatters human pride. In reality, God doesn't need us—not at all. He was doing quite well before we arrived on planet earth, and He won't worry about the future of the world after we leave. The Bible says that He is not "served by human hands, as though He needed anything, since He Himself gives to all people life and breath and all things" (Acts 17:25).

If you think that God needs you, His face will elude you. Seldom is one intimate with a demanding employer or a nagging parent or especially an impatient, oppressive Deity. A legalistic attitude about service fuels the flames of intimacy about as effectively as a wet blanket.

However, an opposite extreme also hinders many from gazing into the face of the Divine Lover. This extreme is sometimes disguised as grace. Some have claimed that by virtue of their freedom in Christ, nothing is left for them to do. In fact, the very word *do* raises a red flag in their minds.

These people may have overreacted to a legalistic past—when service was demanded—by now erring on the opposite extreme. Rather than demanding service, they have denounced it. They have embraced a philosophy of passivity in regard to Christian service.

Neither legalistic activity nor licentious passivity are characteristics of the life to which God calls us. Just because Christians don't *have to* serve to be accepted by our heavenly Father doesn't mean that we won't *want to* serve. Authentic grace motivates us to serve because of our love for Jesus Christ and for our fellow man.

Some Christians have redefined grace, and they quickly react against the slightest mention of behavioral matters. Just try to talk to them about service—they'll tell you about their freedom before you even finish your sentence. Any mention of the value of action sounds like legalism to them. They have overrun the grace-base and don't know it.

Grace shouldn't motivate us to sit down and wait until we can go to heaven. Grace enables us to be all that we are called to be and do all that we are called to do, all by virtue of the life of Christ who indwells us. Grace is active, not static. It isn't a stagnant pond but a river of living water flowing from our innermost being (see John 7:38).

Service and the Spiritual Disciplines

Service is another lens through which you may see the face of the Divine Lover. If you have wandered into either legalism or laziness, you may need to adjust your thinking. Jesus said that He did not come to be served but *to serve* (see Matthew 20:28). *Jesus came to serve.*

Distinguishing between service and law is important. However, this is a book about how you can learn to. see the face of God more clearly. Service can help us learn to see the Father's face.

In a culture where we so easily get caught up in the swift current of our busy lives, service is a spiritual discipline that, like others, requires intentionality. Empty religious activity is not service. It is nothing more than busywork with no eternal value. Authentic Christian service flows from a totally different source than dead religious works.

The Meaning of Service

In describing His own actions, Jesus said, "The Son can do nothing of Himself, unless it is something He sees the Father doing; for whatever the Father does, these things the Son also does in like manner" (John 5:19). Jesus said that His actions were the result of what He saw the Father doing. They came from the vital union He shared with His Father.

Authentic Christian service isn't the performance of certain religious activities. It is the outflow of the divine life that resides within every Christian. Many churches emphasize the doing of service, but the *doing* has no inherent spiritual value unless it stems from our *being* in union with Jesus Christ.

Christian service is Christ's service through the believer. As He rests in His Father and we rest in Him, the union we all share becomes the catalyst for acts of service. Anything else is nothing more than a Pharisaical game of dead religion.

Richard Foster notes:

> Self-righteous service comes through human
> effort. It expends immense amounts of energy

calculating and scheming how to render the service. Sociological charts and surveys are devised so that we can "help those people." True service comes from a relationship with the divine Other deep inside. We serve out of whispered promptings, divine urgings. Energy is expended but it is not the frantic energy of the flesh.[1]

Serving others means letting Jesus Christ live His life through us, expressing His tender love and acceptance toward others by meeting their needs. Two thousand years ago He touched the sick, hugged the lonely, helped the down-and-out, comforted those who mourned, and set free those who were in bondage. Has He changed since those days? If not, He still wants to do those same things through you today.

Christ hasn't lost His compassion for people. He still wants to reach out to the lowest, the least, and the last, to offer Himself to them through meaningful expressions of love. You are the instrument through which He wants to bring that love to others.

Service Motivated by Love

Grace frees many to enjoy serving Christ in an unprecedented way. It moves service from the "ought to" column in our lives into the "want to" column. Service is no longer an obligation but an opportunity.

Only when we serve from grace are we freed from selfish motives. We are finally able to stop trying to score points with God by what we do for Him. For the first time we are free to serve Him, not for any advantage it gives us but simply because we love Him.

An example from my own life has taught me this lesson. When I was 16 years old, I had never been out on a date.

I had wanted to date, and I had even prayed for a girl-friend, but my prayers seemed to fall on deaf ears.

One day I was sitting in my Sunday school class at church when a guest came into the room. I had never seen this pretty girl before, but I decided to start my dating career *right now*. After going home that day and getting permission from my dad to borrow his car for the big date, I counted the hours until the next Sunday. I hoped this girl would come back to church.

The next week, my prayers were answered. She did return. After church, I went out into the parking lot where she was standing. Trying to act as cool as any 16-year-old could be, I started to make my first move. I had never done this before, and I wanted to be smooth. Looking out from under my Beatles haircut, I began...

"Uh...do you, like, have plans this Friday night?" I stammered.

"No, I don't. Why?" the pretty girl answered.

"Well, um...I thought, um...that maybe, if you, uh... wanted to, we could go to a movie and then have a pizza?" I continued.

"Sure, that sounds like fun," the girl answered.

Outwardly, I answered with the most "groovy" demeanor I could muster. "Cool." But inwardly, I was shouting, "Thank you God! I have a date! I have a date!"

When the next Friday came, I couldn't wait to pick up this girl for my first-ever date. I wanted her to like me and was willing to do everything I could think of to make that happen. I washed my dad's car from top to bottom—wax on the outside, upholstery cleaner on the inside. I wore a tie—and cologne—a *lot* of cologne. I even took the bottle with me so that I could do a touch-up right before I picked her up.

I was so anxious that I arrived at her house almost 30 minutes early. I knocked on the door and her mother answered. "She's not quite ready yet," she said. "You're welcome to come in and wait."

"I don't mind waiting at all!" I gushed. I walked into the house where the girl's dad sat, cleaning a shotgun and quietly staring at me.

Finally, the pretty girl came out. I stood to greet her and rushed ahead to open the door for her. I wanted her to like me. I reached the car before her and opened that door too, hoping she would be impressed by my chivalry.

Once we were in the movie theater, it was the *large* Coke and popcorn for her. Then, at the restaurant, I said, "Choose anything you want from the menu. Cost doesn't matter."

At the end of that date, when I took the pretty girl home, she said, "I had a good time."

"You did?" I responded. "I did too. Do you want to go out again next week?"

"Sure," she answered.

I was thrilled. It was my first date, and she had liked me enough to do it again!

I went out with that girl the next Friday. In fact, I went out with her *every* Friday—for three years—then I married her.

Melanie and I married in 1973. Some time later, I thought to myself, *I don't have to open the car door for her now. We're married.* Before, cost in a restaurant hadn't mattered, but now it began to matter. I hadn't minded waiting for her to finish getting ready when we dated, but now I was often impatient.

Conflict increased during the first few years of our marriage. We began to wonder if our marriage would survive. Arguments became more frequent.

I thought that prayer was the only hope we had, so I began to pray alone every night. I always prayed the same prayer: *Lord, you* must *change that woman!* One night, the Lord spoke to me: *No, Steve. I must change you. She isn't*

*perfect, but that's not your responsibility. You just trust Me
to change you.*

Over the months that followed, a miracle occurred. I
was transformed by Christ, and I began to *serve* Melanie—
not to cause her to love me but because I loved her. We've
been married three decades now. Today I open the car
door for her. She can order whatever she wants in the
restaurant. I even make a serious attempt to patiently wait
for her to finish getting ready to go.

My desire is to serve my wife. Not because I want to
impress her but because I love her. That perspective
changed my marriage.

The same kind of change in attitude about service
toward God will transform your Christian life. To gaze into
the face of your Divine Lover, love must be the only motivation for your service. We don't serve Him to get particular results from Him but because we love Him.

Keeping Our Eyes Open

Many believers no longer understand the true nature
of service. The enemy has fooled many into thinking spiritual service is their gift to God. Nothing could be further
from the truth.

Good works are not our gifts to God but rather His gifts
to us! Our heavenly Father has a plan to do some wonderful things in this world and, because of His great love for
us, He has chosen to allow us to participate in that work.
We have already seen that He doesn't need us to do the
work. He chooses to do the work through us because He
loves us.

The apostle Paul said, "For we are His workmanship,
created in Christ Jesus for good works, *which God prepared
beforehand* so that we would walk in them" (Ephesians
2:10, emphasis added). Those who believe that Christian
service is the way we are obligated to glorify God will
never clearly see His lovely face smiling at them with pride.

They will forever be caught in a performance trap, wondering if they are doing enough.

Legalism stresses the duty we have to serve God, but under the new covenant of grace, God has prepared opportunities for us to serve Him with joy. The Bible says that the good works performed by the Christian *have already been prepared in advance.* Our part is to simply enter into those works by faith and with thanksgiving to Him.

Do you want to grow in spiritual service? Don't try to develop your own plan. Instead, begin each day asking the Divine Lover, *What plans do you have for me today?* Then move through your day, with your eyes wide open, looking for the opportunities He has prepared for you to serve Him.

Each time you see a chance to do a good work, consider it to be a gift the Divine Lover has placed in your day as a pleasant surprise. Go through all your days expecting to find the gifts (opportunities) that He has arranged for you. Unwrap every opportunity and see what He has planned. This approach to service turns life into an adventure filled with wonderful and surprising gifts all along the way.

~

LOOKING UPWARD

How are we to recognize the opportunities through which we are called to serve God by serving others? With so many needs in the world, how are we to know which ones we are personally called to meet? Jesus said He did that which He saw His Father doing. How can you know the things that the Father wants to do through you? The following exercises may help you to identify the good works that the Divine Lover has prepared for you as gifts.

1. What past experiences have prepared you to serve
   in a particular way today?

   The Holy Spirit uses our own backgrounds to
   prepare us to serve others. Chuck Colson was known
   as "the hatchet man" in Richard Nixon's adminis-
   tration. He would have never thought of reaching
   out to prison inmates until he *became* an inmate in
   Alabama's Maxwell Prison in 1974. From his own
   painful experiences came the passion to establish
   Prison Fellowship Ministries. Today multitudes of
   lives have been impacted because of his willingness
   to own his past experiences and surrender them to
   a loving God.

   Your own opportunities for service may be related
   to painful experiences in your life. A lady I met in
   one church used to be a crack addict who lived on
   the streets. Today she ministers to the homeless.
   Another friend says that he was a "mean drunk"
   earlier in life. Today he ministers to men struggling
   with an addiction to alcohol. Who can better understand and minister to someone addicted to drugs or
   alcohol than those who have been there themselves?
   Many a young unwed mother has been blessed by
   the ministry of another woman who knew from
   experience what she was going through.

   Don't think that your blemished past has in any
   way disqualified you from powerful Christian service. Our heavenly Father stands above all the faults
   and failures of our lives and is able to weave the
   dark threads of life into the beautiful tapestry of
   ministry He has prepared for each of us. God wasn't
   the source of your past sins, but He is Lord over
   them and may use your past to equip you to share
   His love with people that others could never reach.

   Don't be ashamed of your past. Your sins are
   forgiven. You are free to be transparent about your

life. The Divine Lover has led you safely across rocky terrain, and He may use you to guide others safely across the same area until they too find themselves resting in His loving arms. Pray and ask the Holy Spirit to show you how your past may be a bridge to present ministry.

Write in your notebook past experiences that you thought were best forgotten. Maybe they should never be brought out again, but have you ever prayed and asked the Lord if He wants to use you to assist another person who is traveling the same road? Pray about the things you have written down and ask for guidance.

Perhaps you have underestimated God's ability and desire to reach others through your past weaknesses. The apostle Paul talked about his weaknesses when he had the opportunity to serve others in ministry (see 1 Corinthians 2:3; 2 Corinthians 11:30; 12:9). Maybe your past should be forgotten—maybe not. Pray and listen for an answer.

2. Pray and ask to be sensitive to the needs of others.

"I turn the channel every time I see those starving children," one friend told me. "It is too painful to watch. I can't help them all," he rationalized. At the time, I thought about my own lifestyle. I had to admit that though his remark sounded harsh, I wasn't exactly overflowing with empathy for hurting people myself.

Later, as I thought about our conversation, I asked the Father, *Why don't I have the compassion for people that I know You have?* Instantly, I heard His voice answering in my thoughts, *Because you don't see the things I see.*

That made sense to me. I knew that I lived in a cultural bubble where the suffering of humanity was little more than an abstract concept to me. My home has central heating and air. My family eats three meals a day. I can express my faith with no risk of repercussions. I realized a fact: I've been spoiled.

I don't need to apologize or be self-conscious about God's blessings, but I did recognize the need to be stretched outside my comfort zone. I prayed, *Father, allow me to see some of those things if that's how I can share your heart with the world. I want to hurt over the things that hurt you.*

Within the next few years, the Divine Lover answered that prayer. I wept in India as I stood in a leper colony and spoke to people who were physically wasting away in small increments every day. Many had already lost their nose, ears, toes, fingers. I felt my Father's heartbeat that day as I hugged, kissed, and laid my hands on withering lepers and prayed for them.

I stood in an abandoned factory in China when the temperature was 20 below zero. A family of six lived there with no heat or food and little furnishings. For a week I taught them and their friends the Bible, and they nourished me with their love and faith in Christ. I wept as I listened to numerous stories of persecution these precious saints had suffered. Tears streamed down my cheeks as I told one young mother I could not smuggle her nine-year-old son out of the country and make him my own so that he would have a chance in life.

Pray and ask your Father to allow you to experience His heart for hurting people, and He will answer. You don't have to go to China or India. He can use a visit to a local children's hospital, cancer clinic, homeless shelter, or soup kitchen to accomplish the same thing.

Must you *act* in some way to have your Father's heart toward those who hurt? The Holy Spirit will show you the answer to that question. Do you live in a bubble? If so, the chances are likely that He will lead you to settings where your heart will be touched. Keep your eyes wide open and look for the opportunities to be exposed to hurting people whom you can love.

Service is an intentional spiritual discipline. If you sense the Holy Spirit stirring you in this area, act on the choice to go somewhere, see something, and do something about it. This encouragement isn't intended to make you feel guilty for what you haven't done but to encourage you. You may sense that the Holy Spirit is giving you a *desire* to be stretched so that you might have new and greater opportunities to join Him in the work He is doing in this world. He wants to show the Father's love for hurting people and will allow you to be the messenger. You will find yourself growing in a sense of servanthood as He exposes you to the needs of hurting people.

3. Pray and ask how your own unique skills may be used in Christian service.

Many people underestimate God's ability to use them in service to others. Don't think that God can't use you in ministry because you aren't trained in a specific area. The Divine Lover will use you to express His love to others with whatever abilities He has given you.

What is your profession? Ask God how you may use your career skills at opportune times to show His love to somebody. A friend of mine recently went to heaven. His doctors completely forgave the astronomical medical bills left for the surviving wife.

What a testimony of our Father's faithfulness! I heard of someone else who bought a home that he furnished and makes available to missionaries on furlough.

Don't think that your service has to be something big. Ordinary acts of love are powerful and effective. One of the thrills of our lives happened when Melanie and I "adopted" a person in the small town where we lived. Robert lived in a run-down shack in a poor part of town. We wanted to show him the love of Jesus. We invited him to our home for dinner, took him to church with us, and bought him clothes and groceries. At Christmas we surprised him with a Christmas tree and wrapped gifts. None of the items were expensive, but he was thrilled. But not as much as we were.

Consider the following as simple ways to serve others:

- baby-sitting for a young couple who seldom get a night out

- cooking a meal and taking it to a sick friend

- mowing a neighbor's lawn

- regularly visiting a shut-in

- sending a note of affirmation to a friend

The simple ways that you can serve others are unlimited. Pray and ask the Holy Spirit to show you other ways to serve people and show His love to them. Write down the things He shows you and then make a list of names to correspond with each item on the list. As you follow through with your service, you'll discover that it really is more blessed to give than to receive!

The Divine Lover has prepared gifts for you to enjoy each day as you serve Him by serving others. The spiritual discipline of service is a lens through which you can see His face in the face of others. Go into each day with excitement about the privilege to serve. Keep your eyes wide open, and in the end you may find yourself saying, "Lord, when did we see you hungry, and feed You, or thirsty, and give You something to drink? And when did we see you a stranger, and invite You in, or naked, and clothe you? When did we see you sick, or in prison, and come to You?" Then the Divine Lover will answer and say, "To the extent that you did it to one of these brothers of Mine, even the least of them, you did it to Me" (Matthew 25:37-40).

Dear Father,

I want to know Your heart for the world. Stretch my vision, compassion, and ministry toward others. May I see the world as You see it. Through my service, may Your love richly bless the lives of all those around me. Amen.

9
Celebration:
Knowing Our Lover's Heart

"I THINK GOD IS OUT TO GET ME!" George Castanza once said to Jerry on the popular television sitcom *Seinfeld*.

"I thought you didn't believe in God," Jerry answered.

"I do for the bad stuff!" George replied.

George's comical answer reflects a sad attitude common among many people, including many Christians. Legalistic religion portrays God as perturbed most of the time if not downright angry. After all, when you consider that sin runs rampant in the world, and if you agree that even Christians can't seem to get it right much of the time, why wouldn't God be in a bad mood?

God in a bad mood?

That concept carries some serious implications.

I'm reminded of a T-shirt I saw in a store that read, "If mama ain't happy, ain't nobody happy."

Transfer that viewpoint onto Deity, and we're all in serious trouble! If God *is* in a bad mood, then we had better toe the line because His anger is no small matter. God-sized anger produces God-sized judgment. The Bible says that at the end of time, those who stand in the path of His anger will beg the mountains to fall on them and hide them from His terrible wrath (Revelation 6:16).

To suggest that God isn't in a bad mood doesn't mean that He doesn't care about the things of this world that contradict His holiness. God takes no pleasure in sin. Injustice, cruelty, and all the other sins are affronts to Him and will one day be judged.

On the other hand, God is omniscient and sees from beginning to end. From the eternal perspective, He sees the day when all wrongs will be made right. He will balance all the books in the end.

In regard to the believer, our Heavenly Father has discharged all anger toward our sin at the cross. One day, those who do not know Him will experience the full weight of His wrath against their sin. But for the believer, judgment toward our sin is a moot point. *It is finished*, declared Jesus from the cross. Nothing can change your Father's disposition toward you.

Is God short-tempered? Does His patience wear thin when His children don't act the way they should? Nothing could be further from the truth. If you believe God is in a bad mood, you will have difficulty enjoying the spiritual disciplines and gazing into the face of God. After all, who wants to look into the eyes of somebody who is scowling at them?

Especially if that Person is God.

If you desire genuine intimacy with God, your current understanding of His demeanor may need to be completely dismantled. I'll state the truth as plainly as possible—*God is in a good mood!* He isn't edgy about all that is going on in this world. God doesn't bite His fingernails or take antacids.

The Incarnation

We can know that God is in a good mood because of Jesus. In the incarnation of Christ, we see God running out of heaven toward man with a big smile on His face. In fact, the heavenly realm surrounded the birth of Jesus with jubilant celebration.

One angel shouted with enthusiasm above the others, "I bring you *good* news of *great* joy, which will be for all the people" (Luke 2:10, emphasis added). "Good news of great joy"—that sounds like a reason for a party!

Take note: Jesus performed His first miracle at a wedding party (John 2:1-11). One of the last things He told His disciples before leaving this world was that He wanted them to continue to be full of the joy they had seen in Him (John 15:11). Jesus was a fun-loving person.

If you picture Him as a religious sourpuss, you had better take another look. The people who were attracted to Him were dishonest businessmen, vulgar sailors, prostitutes, and the like—none of which you could exactly call "churchy" people. His opponents, on the other hand, came from a hyper-religious crowd and couldn't crack a smile if their lives depended on it. They challenged Jesus about his lifestyle and He answered them,

> For John the Baptist has come eating no bread and drinking no wine, and you say, "He has a demon!" The Son of Man has come eating and drinking, and you say, "Behold, a gluttonous man and a drunkard, a friend of tax collectors and sinners!" (Luke 7:33-34).

You just can't please Pharisaical, hyper-religious types who love rules more than people. Even Jesus couldn't! Of course we know that Jesus wasn't a glutton and a drunkard, but He obviously wasn't so tightly wound that He didn't enjoy life. He came into this world in the midst of celebration, lived a life of joy (even amidst great sorrow), and on the last night of His life here, challenged the disciples to hold on to that same joy.

Jesus said that He and His Father are one, so we can understand much about the Father by looking at Jesus. Judging from Him, our God isn't a cranky old Deity who doesn't enjoy laughter and joy. To the contrary, He is the ultimate source of celebration and pleasure.

In his book *Orthodoxy,* G.K. Chesterton explains that his examination of pleasure in the world sparked his conversion to Christ. He asserts that the thin veneer of secular materialism he saw in the world offered no satisfying answer for the hope and wonder that exists all around us. Author Barry Morrow writes:

> In [Chesterton's] thinking, only a *romantic* world effused with mystery and awe—like the story of Robinson Crusoe saving goods from his shipwreck—could account for our sense of gratitude and delight in the world. In Chesterton's thinking, the ordinary blessings of life intimate a mysterious world: "I felt in my bones; first, that this world does not explain itself....There was something personal in the world, as in a work of art. I thought this purpose beautiful in its old design."
>
> ...For Chesterton, who was not looking to defend Christian orthodoxy, only Christianity provides a cogent explanation for the existence of pleasure in the world. In his experience and ours, pleasures are Edenic remnants, bits of paradise washed ashore from our ancestral shipwreck.[1]

All pleasure can be ultimately traced to God as its source. A glass of milk that soured because it sat on the counter for three days is no less milk than the milk still in the refrigerator. Both find their origin in the same source, but one has been spoiled by corruption. So it is with the pleasures of life. Sinful pleasures are man's attempt to reach out for what only God can provide. Our heavenly Father is the personification of pleasure. Anything else is sour milk.

The Cross and the Empty Tomb

We can also know that God is in a good mood because of the finished work of Christ. The Bible teaches that Jesus Christ endured the pain and shame of the cross because He knew the joy that was awaiting Him at the right hand of the Father (Hebrews 12:2). The death and resurrection of Jesus Christ is the culmination and focal point of God's plan throughout eternity.

When the stone was rolled away on that first Easter morning, all of heaven must have broken into a spontaneous celebration that hasn't stopped yet. The resurrection of Jesus put a smile on the Father's face that nothing can wipe off. If you could look into heaven at this very instant, you would see everybody praising Jesus Christ for His sacrifice. One day the whole universe will join in the praise.

John saw that day and described it like this:

> Then I looked, and I heard the voice of many angels around the throne and the living creatures and the elders; and the number of them was myriads of myriads, and thousands of thousands, saying with a loud voice, "Worthy is the Lamb that was slain to receive power and riches and wisdom and might and honor and glory and blessing." And every created thing which is in heaven and on the earth and under the earth and on the sea, and all things in them, I heard saying, "To Him who sits on the throne, and to the Lamb, be blessing and honor and glory and dominion forever and ever." And the four living creatures kept saying, "Amen." And the elders fell down and worshiped (Revelation 5:11-14).

There's the final chapter in God's cosmic drama. No wonder He is a joyful God who continually celebrates. If we could hear everything in the eternal realm, we would hear a unified voice reverberating across the universe, "Blessing! And honor! And glory! And power! The Lamb is worthy! *Worthy* is the Lamb!"

The Discipline of Celebration

Remember that the Holy Spirit uses the spiritual disci- · plines to help us experience a deeper sense of intimacy with God than we could otherwise know. We have already learned to gaze into the lovely face of our Father through various other lenses. Let's now consider the wonderful lens of celebration.

A life of celebration can be like a default setting for those who have embraced the incarnation, death, and resurrection of Jesus Christ. The final chapter has been written, and at this very moment, we are on our way home.

Nothing will keep God from accomplishing all that He has prepared for you. The One who has begun a good work in you *will* complete it! (See Philippians 1:6.) Right now, even as you read these words, God is celebrating—so why shouldn't we?

How Do We Celebrate?

Celebration was foundational in the growth of the early church. The second chapter of Acts portrays a group of people who laughed and loved, who shared meals and money, and who took seriously the practice of partying under the direction of God's Spirit. They would have fully affirmed C.S. Lewis's claim that "joy is the serious business of heaven." As a result, multitudes were added to the church (Acts 5:14).

A spirit of carefree, lighthearted, God-centered celebration is often conspicuously absent from the lives of most contemporary Christians. When did we begin to take ourselves so seriously? What urgent matters have we allowed to rob us of our playful spirit? *We are going to live forever.* How important can things really be that won't even be remembered, let alone *matter* a hundred years from now? What are we trying to prove by our stress-filled agendas, and to whom are we trying to prove it? Without a doubt, most of us need to lighten up.

When we don't maintain an attitude of internal joy that rises above external circumstances, the rhythms of grace in our lives become discordant. The music soon stops. Spiritual disciplines become routine, void of life. Instead of a relationship, Christianity becomes a religion, the last thing God would ever want it to be.

How then can we be freed from the death grip this world has on our playful spirit and begin to participate in the party going on in the kingdom of God?

Becoming like a Child

Jesus said that if we are going to receive the gift of kingdom citizenship with all the privileges associated with it, we must become like children (Mark 10:15). Children know far better than adults how to celebrate—how to have fun. This return to a childlike faith can happen only as we daily yield ourselves to the Holy Spirit and ask Him to bring about the change in our lives. *We can't make the change happen, but He can and will.* We simply cooperate by yielding ourselves completely to Him every day.

The Holy Spirit will work in us to recreate a childlike trust in our Father. He never ignores the sincere cry of the Christian who longs to know Him more intimately. As He transforms us, we will once again begin to share several important qualities with children.

Joy in Little Things

Children naturally find a sense of awe and wonder in the most common aspects of life. As children grow, they need more elaborate reasons to celebrate. Have you seen small children at Christmas enjoy playing with a large box as much as they enjoyed playing with the gift inside it?

I remember one Christmas when Melanie and I were very young and very broke. Two of our four children had been born, and both were preschool age. Santa Claus couldn't be generous that year, but what the gifts lacked in value they made up for with size and number.

One item under the tree was a large particleboard toy box filled with brightly colored balloons. On Christmas morning, the kids practically ignored the other, more elaborate gifts from Santa. But they had the time of their lives with that box full of balloons. They eventually moved beyond that stage, but on that Christmas, nothing could have brought them greater pleasure.

Do you remember a time in your life when Jesus was enough? Modern Christians are often like spoiled children who can't be satisfied. Some churches attempt to appease the appetite for cotton-candy religion with a three-ring circus offering everything but a dancing bear.

Fascination with Repetition

Chesterton wrote about this childlike quality within God Himself:

> Because children have abounding vitality, because they are in spirit fierce and free, therefore they want things repeated and unchanged. They always say, "Do it again" and the grown-up person does it again until he is nearly dead. For grown-up people are not strong enough to exult in monotony. But perhaps God is strong enough to exult in monotony. It is possible that God says every morning, "Do it again" to the sun; and every evening, "Do it again" to the moon. It may not be automatic necessity that makes all daisies alike; it may be that God

makes every daisy separately, but has never got tired of making them. It may be that He has the eternal appetite of infancy; *for we have sinned and grown old, and our Father is younger than we.*[2]

"Our Father is younger than we." Do the implications of Chesterton's observation speak to your own life? Have you become *old*, spiritually speaking? Have you lost the wonder of the God-designed routine of your life?

Strength in Joy

Dr. Patch Adams is founder and director of the Gesundheit Institute, a free health facility in operation for 15 years in Arlington, Virginia. Dr. Adams adds to his training as a physician his experience as a street clown. Working with health and mental health professionals, he explores the relationship between humor and therapy using his unique blend of knowledge, showmanship, and hands-on teaching techniques. Dr. Adams explains, "I interpret my experience in life as being happy. I want, as a doctor, to say it does matter to your health to be happy. It may be the most important health factor in your life." He is persuaded that "the most revolutionary act one can commit in our world is to be happy."

A few years ago, a film staring Robin Williams depicted the healing effect that joy has on the children Patch Adams treats. His young patients literally have found physical strength, he believes, in joyful celebration.

Joy often leads to celebration, but it can work the other way around too. The practice of celebration in life can foster a sense of joy. From that joy comes the strength to advance through life.

Another medical example of how a jubilant attitude can bring strength comes from the story of Norman Cousins, who wrote the book *Anatomy of an Illness.* Cousins tells

how he used the therapy of laughter to help him overcome a crippling disease. While lying in a hospital bed,
he watched old episodes of *Candid Camera*. He also
watched old movies by the Marx Brothers. He laid in his
hospital bed and laughed hysterically. His heartfelt belly
laughs had an anesthetic effect on him and allowed him
to sleep, free of pain. Even his doctors confirmed that his
laughter gradually improved his body chemistry.[3]

Nehemiah led the people of Israel to rebuild the wall
around Jerusalem. During a special ceremony celebrating
the project's completion, Ezra, the priest, stood before the
people and began to read the Law of God to them. As he
read, the people were moved to tears, but Nehemiah
encouraged them with these words: "Do not be grieved,
for the joy of the LORD is your strength" (Nehemiah 8:10).

Children naturally find strength in joy. I remember a
joy I experienced as a young boy that generated a sense
of physical strength in me. It was the joy of a new pair
of tennis shoes. Paul Parrot Shoes had the personal guarantee of a talking parrot on a television commercial. Not
only would he give you a free plastic egg filled with candy,
but this parrot assured young customers that his shoes
would "make your feet run faster, as fast as I can fly."

I begged my parents for Paul Parrot Shoes. When I got
those shoes home, I put them on, laced them up, and went
outside to try them out. I timed myself as I ran completely
around my house. It was true! I could *feel* the strength
these shoes were giving me. I imagined that Paul Parrot
himself couldn't keep up if he were flying beside me. I
ran around my house faster than ever. I had never actually timed myself before, but that didn't matter. I just *knew*
this was a record.

Do you want to find strength to "run and not grow
weary" (Isaiah 40:31 NIV)? Then resolve to practice the discipline of celebration. If anybody has a reason to celebrate,
you do. The party in the kingdom of God is going on right

now. Don't be like the older brother in the story of the prodigal son who stood outside and missed the fun. Join the celebration and watch your strength grow.

Joy in Any Circumstance

The apostle Paul wrote, "Rejoice in the Lord always, again I will say, *rejoice!"* (Philippians 4:4, emphasis added). Paul obviously learned the value of celebration because he didn't write these words from a villa on the Mediterranean Sea. He wrote them from a prison cell where the Romans held him for preaching the gospel. Paul had learned to dance to the blues as well as to an upbeat, cheerful melody.

A childlike (not child*ish*) man can celebrate when he is in prison. Normally, a child has an innate sense that regardless of what is going on in the world around them, everything is going to be all right. After all, they reason, their parents have everything under control.

I have vague memories of the Cuban Missile Crisis. I was a young child at the time. I remember our church family storing canned food and bottled water under a stairway inside the church building. The plan was that we would all gather together at church if a missile were to be launched against us.

My young friends and I explored the room under the stairs with the stockpile of food and water. I thought to myself, *This wouldn't be a bad place to stay for a while.* I wasn't worried about the potential danger at hand. I knew something very bad could happen but reasoned that my parents would take care of me. So while adults worried and prayed and collected bottles of water and cans of food, I played without a care in the world.

To rejoice in the Lord doesn't mean we're oblivious to danger, but it does mean we trust in the protection of our Father. Our security rests in Him, not in the outcome of whatever circumstances we may find ourselves. We celebrate *Him,* not what is happening at a given moment in time. Wherever we might be, we find what C.S. Lewis called "patches of Godlight in the woods of our experience."[4] The light of His presence in any circumstance is all the light we need to keep the party going.

Do you want the practice of celebration to be the constant beat within the rhythms of grace operating in your life? The following suggestions may help you in your Godward gaze. Don't be self-conscious about following these. Allow yourself to be stretched beyond your comfort zone.

⁓

LOOKING UPWARD

1. At the end of each day, identify something from the events of the day that you can celebrate.

   Many people collapse with fatigue at the end of their day, just happy that the day is over and eager to rest. Some mentally rehearse the negative things that have happened that day. Practice a lifestyle of celebration by recognizing the many blessings that God gives us every day. Let thanksgiving to God be your last thought at night and your first thought in the morning. You will need to cultivate an attitude of celebration. It doesn't come naturally in our stress-filled, anxiety-ridden society.

2. Sing a song aloud to the Lord.

   Paul and Silas sang to the Lord at midnight in a Philippian jail (Acts 16:25). The Psalmist encourages us to "Come before Him with joyful singing" (Psalm 100:2). A search in a good concordance will show that singing has been a part of intimate interaction with God throughout the history of His people. After all, who do you think created music?

Pick a song that expresses your thoughts and feelings toward Him. Don't sing with a recording. Sing your solo to the Divine Lover. If you can't find a place to sing where you aren't afraid you'll get embarrassed by being heard, wait until you are in the car or sing in the shower as you begin your day. Fix your mind on Him and *sing*. Your emotions might amaze you if you really sing to Him from your heart.

3. Find reasons to laugh at yourself.

Laughing at ourselves is a healthy part of a lifestyle of celebration because it reminds us that life doesn't have to be taken so seriously. To laugh at yourself has the effect of a good dose of medicine. I have often laughed at my own weaknesses— my terrible sense of direction, my pathetic lack of mechanical skills, and many other things that I'm not secure enough to put into print!

Topping the list are the foolish things I have mistakenly said. After I had spoken in one church service, I wanted everybody to stand to their feet and bow their heads for prayer. That's what I *wanted*. What I *said* was, "Will you please stand with your head bowed to your feet?" Later, some people told me that they thought I was beginning some sort of aerobics ministry right there on the spot. We all had a good laugh—especially me.

Learn to laugh at your idiosyncrasies and you'll discover that you can create a refreshingly joyful atmosphere. In your notebook, make a list of the things you can laugh about concerning yourself. If you can't think of anything, either you're perfect or you take life far too seriously. I'll let you make the call.

4. Make a list of fun things to do during the next month.
   Remember that God is the ultimate origin of pleasure. As a loving Father, He takes pleasure in *your*
   pleasure. Schedule some fun time into your life and
   celebrate the blessing of pleasure. See God participating in the activity with you. Gaze into His face
   through your fun. Watch the expression of joy on
   His face. Listen to His laughter of delight as He gives
   you the gift of a good time.

   Don't listen to accusing voices from within that
   suggest you're wasting time. Spending time with
   Jesus is never a waste. Reclaim the wonder you
   knew as a child. Laugh again. Break free from the
   crippling lie that says you must always be serious
   to be spiritual. Let the joy of the Lord fill you. Put
   on your spiritual Paul Parrot grace shoes and run,
   skip, and jump again!

This earth-life will be over soon. If you're going to learn
how to dance before you are ushered into the Big Ballroom,
you had better practice now. Heaven is a party, and earth
is a classroom where you can learn to sing and dance so
that you won't have to be a wallflower in eternity.

The apostle Paul said it like this: "Celebrate God all day,
every day. I mean, *revel* in Him!" (Philippians 4:4 THE
MESSAGE). Are you reveling in the celebration of your life
in Christ all day, every day? That's what the Bible tells us
to do!

My granddaughter, Hannah, was in a ballet recital a few
years ago, along with other four-year-old girls. As she
danced, she did the same thing I had seen her mother do
many years earlier when she was in a public performance.
She looked for her parents (and in this case, also her
grandparents—at least that's what I'm choosing to believe).

When she caught the eye of her parents and us, we
were all reacting in the same way. We were smiling—big.

We were thrilled to see her dance. Her joy in dancing was only surpassed by our own.

Do you believe we love Hannah more than your heavenly Father loves you?

Go ahead. Make Him proud.

Get up and dance with life.

Dear Father,

I want to dance with life again. I want to know the awe of childlike faith and the wonder of living in a world where You control every detail. Save me from an adult mentality that squelches my faith. Show me how to live with the carefree abandon of a child. I want to sing and dance and laugh and run with You. Grow me, Father, so that I will mature into a child again, one who can enjoy Your kingdom to the fullest. Amen.

10
20/20 Vision

I'LL NEVER FORGET THE DAY I FINALLY DECIDED I needed reading glasses. I was sitting in a restaurant booth across from a friend. As I tried in vain to read the menu, I held it at arm's length. My friend across the table asked with a knowing smile, "Are you trying to show me something?"

"No," I laughed. "I'm trying to get this thing far enough away to see it."

"Here, try these," he said, reaching across the table to hand me his reading glasses.

I was amazed at how clearly I could see. I brought the menu back to my side of the table, where I could now easily read it. Immediately after lunch, I headed for the dollar store, where I bought several pairs of those new eyes.

I would never have known just how poor my vision was or how much reading glasses could help me if I hadn't been willing to try on my friend's glasses. Once I did try them on, I knew that the lens he used was exactly what I needed too. I knew I didn't want to live without them anymore.

That's how the spiritual disciplines have worked in my life.

For a long time, I couldn't relate at all to words like *contemplation* or *meditation* or some of the other terms presented in this book.

Then the time came when friends began to share how much clearer they could see the Lord through the lenses of the spiritual disciplines. At first I thought I didn't need their prescription. However, the Holy Spirit kept bringing people, books, tapes, and other voices into my life that all echoed the same message: Spiritual disciplines will help you see more clearly!

I began to try them on, and just as they had said, I *could* see Jesus better. That's what prompted me to write this book. Jesus is using these wonderful rhythms of grace to help me see, just as He has helped other Christians in centuries past.

I hope that as you have read *The Godward Gaze,* you've tried on the lenses presented here. Perhaps they don't sell these glasses at the store where you normally shop. That's okay. Churches are each strong in different areas.

I grew up in a mainline evangelical church where I wasn't taught the spiritual disciplines. That is not a negative reflection on my upbringing, for I learned things there that have sustained and guided me throughout my life. No church or group has a corner on the truth. We are interdependent on each other in the body of Christ.

Sadly, many Christians can learn from somebody who lived in another century but can't learn from somebody living right now who happens to attend a different church. Let's learn to encourage each other to see the face of God. To do so, however, we must be open to changes in our own perspective.

Do you want to see the Divine Lover more clearly? Are you willing to try on the lenses of the spiritual disciplines? This may require a change in the way you pray, read your

Bible, listen to music or watch movies, and perform other activities in your life.

Are you willing to change?

I once had a conversation with a friend who boasted that he hadn't changed since we started out together in ministry decades earlier.

"Do you see that as a *virtue?*" I asked him. Growing things always change. I trust that you've read this book because you want God to bring about change in your life in some way.

In the introduction, I quoted 2 Corinthians 3:18, where the Bible says we are changed into the image of the Lord by beholding Him—by gazing steadfastly into His loving face. The preceding chapters have been a prescription for lenses through which your view of the Divine Lover may become clearer and more sharply focused. Maybe you already wore some of the lenses prescribed here. I hope that you have begun to try on others for the first time.

Several vision problems exist in the church today that can prevent Christians from clearly seeing Jesus through the spiritual disciplines. As we come to the close of *The Godward Gaze,* open yourself to the Great Physician and allow Him to show you whether you have one of the following problems with your own spiritual sight.

Blindness

Jesus encountered many people who were physically blind during His earthly ministry. However, He called only two groups spiritually blind. One was the Pharisees. Unfortunately, this group believed with all their hearts that they saw things more clearly than everybody else. (Modern Pharisees still believe that.)

What caused their spiritual blindness? Legalism. Perhaps nothing obscures a clear vision of the face of the Divine Lover as does legalism. This malady is dangerously difficult to recognize because it develops gradually.

When I had my eyes examined a few years ago, the optometrist gave me a warning as she looked into the pupil of my left eye. "This eye has something that you shouldn't be worried about now, but at some point it will need attention," she said.

"What is it?" I asked.

"I see the very early stages of a cataract in this eye," she answered.

"A cataract?!" I asked in disbelief. "At *my* age?"

The optometrist continued, "This isn't something to worry about now. It will probably take it 20 years to grow to the point where you'll need to have something done about it. I'm just telling you so that you can have it checked over the years."

Legalism and Blindness

Some Christians begin their new life in Christ with perfect vision. However, as time progresses, legalism, like a cataract, begins to gradually grow in their spiritual vision until it eventually blinds them to the presence of Jesus Christ. Intellectually, they know He is there, but they gradually lose their *experiential* sight of Him. They talk about times they have seen Him in the past, but they have completely lost sight of Him actively working in their lives today. They have, as Jesus said about one church, "lost their first love."

Remember that I defined the spiritual disciplines as, "biblical practices, *motivated by love* and practiced in faith, that help us experience a deeper sense of intimacy with God than we could otherwise know." Legalism suffocates love and cuts us off from the very life force of the spiritual disciplines.

Sometimes people with failing vision pretend to see better than they do. That's what a Christian legalist does. In an effort to keep up appearances, those blinded by legalism contend that they can see clearly. They go through religious motions, but with each passing day their view of the Divine Lover's face grows dimmer. Those actions that were once animated by His indwelling life and motivated by love now become religious routine. Legalists have traded a Person for performance.

They read the Bible, but it doesn't read them. They say prayers but don't pray. They watch and listen but no longer see and hear. They tell everybody around them how to walk but don't know where they are going themselves. They are "blind guides of the blind" (Matthew 15:14).

The source of legalists' behavior is not love for Jesus Christ but dead, religious duty. They believe they gain God's favor by what they do. They miss the point altogether that behavior isn't what brings God pleasure. God is pleased only by *faith* (Hebrews 11:6).

Those blinded by legalism typically get hung up on the technicalities of religious rules, but they have lost sight of the things that are really important. They argue over incidentals that have no eternal value. They are missing Jesus!

Jesus spoke to them in Matthew 23. Eugene Peterson describes the scene in *The Message,* when Jesus said to them,

> You're hopeless, you religion scholars and Pharisees! Frauds! You keep meticulous account books, tithing on every nickel and dime you get, but on the meat of God's Law, things like fairness and compassion and commitment—the absolute basics!—you carelessly take it or leave it. Careful bookkeeping is commendable, but the basics are required. Do you have any idea how silly you look, writing a life story that's wrong from start to finish, nitpicking over commas and semicolons?

Throughout Matthew 23, Jesus denounces the Pharisees' legalism. Their obsession with rules and indifference to relationships was definitive evidence of their blindness. Jesus said they were missing the whole point.

Christian Legalist?

Have you become blinded by legalism? Some might argue that a Christian can't be a legalist. They understand the word to refer only to those who hope to become a Christian by their works. Although that certainly is one expression of legalism, it isn't the only way a person can act as a legalist.

The apostle Paul wrote his epistle to the Galatians because of the threat of legalism in their church. False teachers had come into the fellowship there, teaching these young Christians that they needed to embrace Christ *and* the law. Paul wrote to them to say, "No! Your life isn't built around the law! Your life is in Jesus Christ!" He asked them, "Did you receive the Spirit by the works of the Law, or by hearing with faith?" (Galatians 3:2).

Paul wasn't writing to them because he was concerned that they might misunderstand salvation. He *knew* they had believed the gospel and received God's Spirit. How could they become confused about the way to become a Christian? They had already become Christians! His concern for them was that, *as Christians,* they might become ensnared in legalism.

The Pharisees were not believers in Christ. The Galatians were. Believers and nonbelievers can be legalists.

Lukewarm Blindness

The second group Jesus called blind were those in the church at Laodicea—the lukewarm church (Revelation 3:14-22). This church clearly demonstrated the effect of legalism. They were in No-Man's Land—not out in the world living in gross sin, but not passionately in love with Jesus anymore.

With a lukewarm heart, we begin to depend on our own self-sufficiency instead of the Divine Lover's indwelling life. The church at Laodicea kept right on with their normal routine. They had actually come to believe that they were fine because they kept going through the motions. They thought they needed nothing, but Jesus said, "You are blind."

The Great Physician stands ready to heal those who are blind. If the Holy Spirit has enabled you to see yourself in this short description of spiritual blindness, the Divine Lover wants to heal you. He delights in healing spiritual blindness. The spiritual disciplines are lenses through which one may gaze into the face of the Divine Lover, but lenses do no good for a person who is blind.

Once, when Jesus was leaving the city of Jericho, two blind men who were sitting on the side of the road heard Jesus coming and cried out to Him, "Have mercy on us, Son of David!" The Bible says, "Moved with compassion, Jesus touched their eyes; and immediately they regained their sight and followed him" (Matthew 20:34).

The good news for the spiritually blind today is that Jesus hasn't lost His sense of compassion. Those who will call upon Him, He will heal of the terrible blindness of legalism and lukewarmness that prevents them from gazing on His beauty. By His grace, they can once again gaze into His lovely face.

Nearsightedness

Nearsightedness is another problem that prevents us from seeing our Father's loving face. To be nearsighted is to be able to see only what is in our face. It isn't the same as blindness because a nearsighted person can see some things. The problem is that he can only see things that are right in front of him.

Who is the nearsighted Christian? It's the person who can't see beyond his religious activity and enjoy genuine intimacy with Christ. In our contemporary church world, which often seems to be built on programs and preachers more than on the Person of Jesus Christ, the danger of nearsightedness is very real.

The problem with nearsightedness is that you can still function. A nearsighted person can pretty much live a normal routine. The only time his vision becomes a problem is if he is trying to see something beyond his immediate space.

That seems to be the problem of many Christians today. Have you gradually lost sight of Jesus Christ? I was startled when I began to realize that I had lost a clear focus on Jesus and had become more preoccupied with the activities of ministry than with Jesus Christ Himself. Many Christians have fallen into this subtle trap.

If you do your daily Bible reading but don't hear the voice of Jesus, you may be nearsighted. If you teach a Bible study class, but the Holy Spirit doesn't teach you, you may be nearsighted. If you sing in the choir without a song in your heart, you may be nearsighted. If you preach sermons but don't have a message from God, you may be nearsighted.

Do you see the symptoms that go with this problem? The tendency to become more caught up with Christian work than with Christ is a universal vulnerability for believers. We can become nearsighted and not know it because we still seem to function okay. However, if we stop long enough to have a spiritual examination, the Holy Spirit will show us that we have a problem.

Unlike a spiritually blind person, the nearsighted person can experience miraculous results if he will apply the spiritual disciplines in his life. A spiritually blind person must be miraculously healed of self-sufficiency and pride before he can begin to embrace the spiritual disciplines. Until he is healed, he won't *want* to see the face of God.

A nearsighted Christian is different. His problem isn't that he is proud or doesn't want to see the face of the Divine Lover. His problem is simply that he gradually has lost his focus on Jesus. He can only see the religious activity right under his nose. He needs the healing touch that the rhythms of grace can bring into his life.

If the Great Physician is showing you that you have become nearsighted, be assured that your vision can be corrected with the lenses of the spiritual disciplines. Have you gradually become more focused on church life and religious activities than on Jesus? Have you lost the sense of joy that you once knew by staring into His face? Do you desire to have your vision restored so that your focus is directly on Christ again?

The awareness of this problem and the desire for change is evidence that the Holy Spirit is speaking to you. Without Him you wouldn't even be aware that you have a need. If He is showing you a need for change in your life, His intent is not to make you feel guilty but to make you aware of what He wants to do in your life. The Great Physician wants to help you so that your vision is restored and you can clearly see Him again.

When I bought contact lenses, the optometrist said, "These won't feel right in your eyes for a few days. You aren't used to having a lens on your eyeball, and you will take a little while to grow accustomed to them. Be patient, and in a short time, you won't feel any discomfort with them at all."

That's how the spiritual disciplines work. Each of the disciplines is a lens through which you may more clearly see the face of the Divine Lover. However, as you begin to wear them, you may feel uncomfortable with them at first. That's normal.

Quietness may be uncomfortable to you. Contemplation may seem awkward. Meditation may feel forced and unnatural. Celebration may feel silly. The disciplines may not seem to fit you at first. Don't give up. Keep wearing these spiritual lenses until you begin to realize a difference in your vision of Jesus. A legalistic sense of duty will not motivate you to practice the spiritual disciplines. Your desire to see Him more clearly will motivate you to keep putting on these corrective lenses every day.

Farsightedness

Farsightedness exists when people can only see something far away. They have problems with a clear focus on the things in close proximity. Spiritual farsightedness is a common problem that, like nearsightedness, will distort our ability to clearly see the face of Jesus Christ.

Those with spiritual farsightedness don't recognize the nearness of Jesus in their daily lives. The authenticity of their faith isn't in question, but they miss the joy of intimacy with Christ because they're looking past Him to other things. Like those who are nearsighted, they may be sincere, but they don't recognize the closeness of the indwelling Christ.

A spiritually farsighted person is sometimes more caught up with biblical information than intimacy with Jesus. He may go to church with a notebook in his hand to take sermon notes. He might be well-versed in the knowledge of Scripture and able to intelligently discuss the fine points of theology.

He may attend seminars on apologetics, prophecy, eschatology, or other topics that go deep into the Word. His shelves at home may be filled with notebooks, study guides, Bible commentaries, and dictionaries. He might even know how to study the original languages of the Scripture.

Nothing is wrong with any of these things. In fact, these can be good *unless* they have become substitutes for genuine intimacy with Jesus Christ. If you're the type of person who really enjoys the academic aspects of life— if you like to dig in deep and learn everything you can about a subject—you may be vulnerable to spiritual farsightedness.

Gaining information is much easier than nurturing intimacy in a relationship. However, all the knowledge we can accumulate about the Bible is no substitute for experiencing intimacy with Jesus Christ. Christianity is, above all, a love relationship. When we choose information instead of intimacy, we miss the heart of Christianity. Jesus didn't die so that you could know something. He died so that you could know *Him.*

Another sign of spiritual farsightedness is a preoccupation with biblical principles rather than with the Person of Christ. The contemporary church often stresses the need to live by principles. That emphasis especially appeals to those who have a bent toward discipline and regiment.

Many people want a formula for a life of faith. Give them a recipe for right living, and they'll commit themselves to follow it to the letter of the law. Some thrive on a checklist that allows them to keep constant watch on how well they are doing in their walk.

But relationships don't work that way. What would you say if someone asked you, "What are the main principles you live by in your relationship to your mate?" or, "What principles do you use to love your children?" Your first response to them would probably be, "What do you mean?" You wouldn't understand because you don't use principles to relate to your family. You relate to them in love.

Do you recognize the symptoms of spiritual farsightedness in your life? If so, the Great Physician may use the prescription of the spiritual disciplines to restore your vision of Him. Do you remember the passion of the relationship you had with Jesus when you first met Him? The Divine Lover wants to restore that sense of passionate intimacy.

Living with 20/20 Vision

The Godward gaze is about staring into the face of One who loves us with an infinite love. Spiritual disciplines are helpful in providing practical ways that we can see Him clearly. The disciplines aren't obligations to be embraced. They are opportunities to be enjoyed!

So many things in the world today have the potential of blurring our vision of the Divine Lover. We can easily be distracted, focusing in the wrong places. When we lose sight of His lovely face, everything in life becomes disheveled even though we might appear to be moving through our days in an orderly way. Through the spiritual disciplines, we can gain 20/20 vision.

When I allowed myself to become caught up in the demands of life, I noticed that I had lost my focus on Jesus again. I had allowed the demands of life to temporarily blur my spiritual vision. I am still receiving treatment for this spiritual malady from the Great Physician.

One morning as I sat at my desk thinking about the many duties I needed to do that day, I paused. I wrote the following sentence in my journal: "In the midst of my frenzied days and restless nights, I hear a tender voice within me gently whispering, *Come home.*"

As I read my own words, my eyes filled with tears. At that moment, I turned my undivided attention to my heavenly Father and saw His face in the deepest part of my spirit. He was smiling, lovingly. In my mind, I laid my head against Him as He hugged away the stress of life. I gazed into His eyes, which glistened with tears of joy because I belong to Him. And I softly wept.

Gazing into your Father's face—no other experience is like it.

In His face you will find healing and hope.

From His loving eyes come holiness and harmony for your life. As you stare into those eyes, which will never look away from you for all eternity, everything becomes clear.

Do you want to see Him?

Then stare deeply into His eyes. He has been looking at you all the time, waiting for you to make eye contact. When you're looking at Him, you'll discover that you never want to look away.

Notes

A Mistaken Identity

1. Richard Foster, *Celebration of Discipline* (New York: HarperCollins Publishers, 1998), 9-11.

Chapter 2—Quietness: Hearing Our Lover's Voice

1. Henri Nouwen, *The Only Necessary Thing* (New York: The Crossroad Publishing Company, 1999), 82.

2. *Ibid.,* 42-43.

Chapter 3—Contentment: Living from a Satisfied Heart

1. Malcolm Muggeridge, *Jesus Rediscovered* (New York: Doubleday, 1979), 179.

2. C.S. Lewis, *The Quotable Lewis* (Wheaton, IL: Tyndale House, 1989), 99.

3. Barry Morrow, *Heaven Observed* (Colorado Springs, CO: NavPress, 2001), 48-49.

4. Many years ago I heard Jack Taylor speak about this text in Scripture. I took his observations and, over the years, have added my own thoughts. At this point, I can't remember what came from where, but I do want to acknowledge his strong influence on my thinking about this subject.

Chapter 4—Contemplation: Idleness with the Almighty

1. Eugene Peterson, *The Contemplative Pastor* (Carol Stream, IL: Word Publishing, 1989), 33.

2. Tony Horsfall, *The Call To Intimacy* (London, England: Share The Word Publications, 2001), 123.

3. *Ibid.*

4. Henri Nouwen, *The Only Necessary Thing* (New York: The Crossroad Publishing Company, 1999), 110.

5. *Ibid.*, 83.

6. John Ortberg, *The Life You've Always Wanted* (Grand Rapids: Zondervan, 1997), 135.

7. Barry Morrow, *Heaven Observed* (Colorado Springs, CO: NavPress, 2001), 61. Quoting an essay entitled *The Scrolls* by Woody Allen.

Chapter 5—Meditation: Bathing in His Word

1. *The Confessions of Saint Augustine,* translated by Rex Warner (New York, Signet Books, 1960).

2. Richard Foster, *Celebration of Discipline* (New York: HarperCollins Publishers, 1998), 29.

3. Tony Horsfall, *The Call To Intimacy,* 110.

4. Richard Foster, *Celebration of Discipline,* 27.

5. *Ibid.*, 23.

6. Madame Guyon, *Exploring the Depth of Jesus Christ* (Goleta, CA: Christian Books, 1975), 16.

7. Richard Foster, *Celebration of Discipline*, 29.

8. *Ibid.*, 30.

Chapter 6—Identification: Living in Union

1. C.S. Lewis, *Mere Christianity* (New York: Macmillan Publishing, 1978), 64-65.

2. Ian Thomas, *The Saving Life of Christ* (Grand Rapids, MI: Zondervan Publishing, 1972), 120.

3. For a more complete explanation of the nature of man, read chapter three in my book *Grace Walk*, published by Harvest House Publishers, 1995.

4. Calvin, *Institutes*, IV, 17, 32.

5. Martin Luther's Preface to Romans, translated by Brother Andrew Thornton.

Chapter 7—Creativity: An Unassuming Voice

1. Henri Nouwen, *The Return of the Prodigal Son* (New York: Doubleday, 1992), 139.

2. C.S. Lewis, *The Weight of Glory and Other Addresses* (Grand Rapids, MI: Eerdmans, 1949).

Chapter 8—Service: Keeping Our Eyes Wide Open

1. Richard Foster, *Celebration of Discipline*, 128.

Chapter 9—Celebration: Knowing Our Lover's Heart

1. Barry Morrow, *Heaven Observed*, 160.

2. John Ortberg, *The Life You've Always Wanted*, 65.

3. Richard Foster, *Celebration of Discipline*, 198.

4. C.S. Lewis, *Mere Christianity*, 184.

Bibliography

Foster, Richard. *Celebration of Discipline*. New York: HarperCollins Publishers, 1998.

———. *Freedom of Simplicity*. New York: HarperCollins Publishers, 1981.

Horsfall, Tony. *The Call to Intimacy*. London, England: Share The Word Publications, 2001.

Lewis, C.S. *The Weight of Glory and Other Addresses*. Grand Rapids, MI: Eerdmans Publishing Company, 1949.

Morrow, Barry. *Heaven Observed*. Colorado Springs, CO: NavPress, 2001.

Nouwen, Henri J.M. *The Way of the Heart*. New York: Ballantine Books, 1985.

———. *The Only Necessary Thing*. New York: The Crossroad Publishing Company, 1999.

———. *The Return of the Prodigal Son*. New York: Doubleday, 1992.

Ortberg, John. *The Life You've Always Wanted*. Grand Rapids, MI: Zondervan, 1997.

Peterson, Eugene. *The Contemplative Pastor*. Carol Stream, IL: Word Publishing, 1989.

Thomas, Gary. *Seeking the Face of God*. Eugene, OR: Harvest House Publishers, 1999.

Willard, Dallas. *The Spirit of the Disciplines*. New York: HarperCollins Publishers, 1988.

———. *The Divine Conspiracy*. San Francisco: HarperSanFrancisco, 1998.

A Personal Word

If *The Godward Gaze* has impacted your life, I would be happy to hear from you. You can contact me through my website at www.gracewalk.org. There you will find more information about Grace Walk Ministries as well as audio teachings, articles, information about other books I have written, and a listing of my audio/video teaching series. You may also request information by calling 1-800-GRACE-11 or by writing me.

Dr. Steve McVey
Grace Walk Ministries
P.O. Box 31139-9368
Atlanta, Georgia 31139-9368

May the Divine Lover continue to bless you in your own Godward gaze and may you "be able to comprehend with all the saints what is the breadth and length and height and depth, and to know the love of Christ which surpasses knowledge, that you may be filled up to all the fullness of God" (Ephesians 3:18-19).